T0181177

Lecture Notes in Business Information Processing 505

Series Editors

Wil van der Aalst, *RWTH Aachen University, Aachen, Germany*

Sudha Ram, *University of Arizona, Tucson, AZ, USA*

Michael Rosemann, *Queensland University of Technology, Brisbane, QLD, Australia*

Clemens Szyperski, *Microsoft Research, Redmond, WA, USA*

Giancarlo Guizzardi, *University of Twente, Enschede, The Netherlands*

LNBIP reports state-of-the-art results in areas related to business information systems and industrial application software development – timely, at a high level, and in both printed and electronic form.

The type of material published includes

- Proceedings (published in time for the respective event)
- Postproceedings (consisting of thoroughly revised and/or extended final papers)
- Other edited monographs (such as, for example, project reports or invited volumes)
- Tutorials (coherently integrated collections of lectures given at advanced courses, seminars, schools, etc.)
- Award-winning or exceptional theses

LNBIP is abstracted/indexed in DBLP, EI and Scopus. LNBIP volumes are also submitted for the inclusion in ISI Proceedings.

Peter Bludau · Rudolf Ramler · Dietmar Winkler ·
Johannes Bergsmann
Editors

Software Quality
as a Foundation
for Security

16th International Conference on Software Quality, SWQD 2024
Vienna, Austria, April 23–25, 2024
Proceedings

Springer

Editors
Peter Bludau (iD)
fortiss GmbH
Munich, Germany

Dietmar Winkler (iD)
Austrian Center for Digital Production
(CDP) & TU Wien
Vienna, Austria

Rudolf Ramler (iD)
Software Competence Center Hagenberg
GmbH
Hagenberg, Austria

Johannes Bergsmann
Software Quality Lab GmbH
Linz, Austria

ISSN 1865-1348   ISSN 1865-1356 (electronic)
Lecture Notes in Business Information Processing
ISBN 978-3-031-56280-8   ISBN 978-3-031-56281-5 (eBook)
https://doi.org/10.1007/978-3-031-56281-5

Message from the General Chair

The *Software Quality Days* (SWQD) conference and tools fair was first organized in 2009 and has since grown to become Europe's largest annual industry-oriented conference on software quality, with a strong and vibrant community. The program of the SWQD conference was designed to encompass a stimulating mixture of practice-oriented presentations, scientific presentations of new research topics, tutorials, and an exhibition area for tool vendors in the software quality field.

This professional symposium and conference offered a range of valuable opportunities for professional development, new ideas, and networking. Attendees benefited from a series of keynote speeches, professional lectures, exhibits, and tutorials.

The SWQD conference welcomes all who are interested in the wide range of topics related to software quality: software process and quality managers, software testers, test managers, product managers, agile masters, project managers, software architects, software designers, requirements engineers, user interface designers, software developers, IT managers, release managers, development managers, application engineers, DevOps experts, and many more.

The guiding conference topic of SWQD 2024 was "*Software Quality as a Foundation for Security*"; changed product, process, and service requirements, e.g., distributed engineering projects, mobile applications, involvement of heterogeneous disciplines and stakeholders, extended application areas, and new technologies include new challenges and require new and adapted methods and tools to master the constantly increasing needs and expectations for quality and security in software systems and applications.

SWQD 2024 was organized by fortiss GmbH (Munich, Germany), Software Competence Center Hagenberg GmbH (Hagenberg, Austria), Center for Digital Production GmbH (Vienna, Austria), TU Wien, Institute of Information Systems Engineering (Vienna, Austria), and Software Quality Lab GmbH (Linz, Austria).

April 2024   Johannes Bergsmann

Message from the Scientific Program Chairs

The 16th *Software Quality Days* (SWQD) conference and tools fair brought together researchers and practitioners from business, industry, and academia working on quality assurance and quality management for software engineering and information technology. The SWQD conference is one of the largest software quality conferences in Europe.

Over the past years, we received a growing number of scientific contributions to the SWQD symposium. Starting back in 2012, the SWQD symposium included a dedicated scientific program published in scientific proceedings. In this eleventh such edition, we received an overall number of 16 high-quality submissions from researchers across the entire globe, which were each peer-reviewed by 3 or more reviewers in a single-blind review. Out of these submissions, we selected 7 contributions as full papers, yielding an acceptance rate of 44%. Further, we accepted 2 short papers representing promising research directions to spark discussions between researchers and practitioners on promising work in progress.

The main topics from academia and industry focused on Systems and Software Quality Management Methods, Improvements of Software Development Methods and Processes, the latest trends and emerging topics in Software Quality and Security, and Testing and Software Quality Assurance.

To support dissemination and collaboration with practitioners, scientific presentations were integrated into topic-oriented practical tracks. This book is structured according to topics following the guiding conference topic "*Software Quality as a Foundation for Security*":

- Requirements Engineering
- Software Quality
- Continuous Integration and Deployment
- Communication and Collaboration
- Artificial Intelligence
- Security and Compliance

April 2024

Peter Bludau
Rudolf Ramler
Dietmar Winkler

Organization

Organizing Committee

General Chair

Johannes Bergsmann   Software Quality Lab GmbH, Austria

Scientific Program Co-chairs

Peter Bludau   fortiss GmbH, Germany
Rudolf Ramler   Software Competence Center Hagenberg GmbH, Austria
Dietmar Winkler   Austrian Center for Digital Production (CDP) GmbH and TU Wien, Austria

Proceedings Chair

Dietmar Winkler   Austrian Center for Digital Production (CDP) GmbH and TU Wien, Austria

Organizing and Publicity Chair

Petra Bergsmann   Software Quality Lab GmbH, Austria

Program Committee

Silvia Bonfanti   University of Bergamo, Italy
Matthias Book   University of Iceland, Iceland
Maya Daneva   University of Twente, The Netherlands
Deepak Dhungana   University of Applied Sciences, Krems, Austria
Oscar Dieste   Universidad Politécnica de Madrid, Spain
Michael Felderer   German Aerospace Center (DLR), Germany
Henning Femmer   Qualicen GmbH, Germany
Stefan Fischer   Software Competence Center Hagenberg, Austria
Gordon Fraser   University of Passau, Germany
Volker Gruhn   University of Duisburg-Essen, Germany

Contents

Security and Compliance

Requirements Engineering

A Process Proposal for Requirements Engineering for Third-Party Products and a Preliminary Evaluation at Munich Re

Marcel Koschinsky[1,2]([✉]), Henning Femmer[1,3][iD], and Claudia Schindler[2]

[1] South Westfalia University of Applied Sciences, Hagen, Germany
{koschinsky.marcel,femmer.henning}@fh-swf.de, mkoschinsky@munichre.com
[2] Munich Re, Munich, Germany
cschindler@munichre.com
[3] Qualicen GmbH, Coesfeld, Germany
henning.femmer@qualicen.de

Abstract. *Context:* When in need for a software solution, companies of all sizes prefer buying an existing commercial-off-the-shelf (COTS) product rather than investing the time and effort on developing and maintaining their own. However, purchasing the wrong COTS solution can lead to a painful and company-critical process as well. *Problem:* Within this context, the absence of a both repeatable as well as pragmatic approach for the selection of a suitable third-party tool remains a common problem at various companies, including Munich Re. *Approach:* To this end, this work combines and extends established methodologies aiming for an efficient and effective requirements engineering approach. To validate feasibility of the approach, we furthermore report on a pilot study at Munich Re, in which we exemplarily apply the process in-vivo for selecting a requirements modeling tool suggested to be used across all development teams of the whole organization. *Results:* The application at Munich Re indicates the feasibility of the approach for the selection of a medium sized software solution. *Impact:* We encourage practitioners to extend the presented method and incorporate it into their own decision-making process for third-party tools, with the aim to making buy-decisions more objective and more efficient in the future.

Keywords: Requirements Engineering · Third Party Software · Commercial-of-the-shelf (COTS) Software

1 Introduction

In the digitized age, companies rely on IT systems to manage both their core as well as supporting processes. For each of these IT systems, IT management needs to make "Make-or-buy" decisions: Choosing "Make" leads to risky (in terms of time, money, quality) projects, yet enables to create a highly tailored,

P. Bludau et al. (Eds.): SWQD 2024, LNBIP 505, pp. 3–17, 2024.
https://doi.org/10.1007/978-3-031-56281-5_1

fitting product. Due to these risks, there is a growing trend in acquiring software as third-party solutions for business processes [1], emphasizing the importance of the decision-making process between in-house development and external procurement [2]. Furthermore, collaboration with third-party providers offers access to top-notch expertise in process support [2]. As a result, a company can increasingly focus on its core competencies, save potential high resources for in-house development, and provide timely optimization of processes [3]. Despite the advantages these third-party products provide, potential challenges may arise, such as integration into the existing IT landscape or ensuring compliance with security standards [4]. To harness the potential benefits of complementary tools while assessing associated risks, companies need a standardized vendor and product evaluation methodology.

As one example of this situation, Munich Re strategically makes "Make or Buy" decisions, where the decision for "make" is exclusively reserved for daily reinsurance operations. Consequently, applications supporting various processes are procured or licensed from external sources. At Munich Re, there was no standardized, systematic approach in the software development lifecycle to evaluate a tool based on its specific requirements. This paper introduces a practical approach through a Munich Re business case to enhance the assessment of third-party solutions. By addressing company-specific challenges, the paper contributes to the development of an effective methodology for the utilization of third-party products in businesses, using Munich Re as a pilot study.

1.1   Research Questions and Contributions

The general research goal for this stream of work is to create a systematic, i.e. reproducible, process, that makes a buy decision more effective (i.e. less selections of the wrong tool) and more efficient (i.e. less invested resources, existing resources focusing on the necessary work effort). This paper takes a first, preliminary step towards this goal by providing two contributions:

Contribution C1: A formalization of a pragmatic[1] process, as a combination of existing methods.

Contribution C2: A first feasibility study on the selection of a modeling tool potentially to be used by a multitude of projects in the context of Munich Re, the largest reinsurance company worldwide [5].

1.2   Structure of This Paper

We start from the problem statement and the relevance of the topic, leading to a definition of the research questions. Section 2 analyzes related works and identifies the research gap, which this paper aims to address. Afterwards, in

---

[1] In this context, *pragmatic* refers to our focus on applicability within a industrial context. Each steps needs to be executable within a realistic scope and by every regular requirements engineer at Munich Re.

Sect. 3, we formalize the process thereby contributing C1. This process is then empirically evaluated in a feasibility study described in the subsequent Sect. 4, contributing C2. This section describes the context, the approach of the study, the results and finishing with a critical discussion of the results and the threats to validity. The work finishes with a summary and outlook to future work in Sect. 5.

2 Background and Related Work

In this section, we conduct a comprehensive analysis encompassing both the state of the art and the state of the practice concerning third-party tool selection approaches. Subsequently, we derive a research gap based on our observations from this examination.

2.1 State of the Art

Several efforts have been dedicated to advancing the research goal mentioned in the realm of Requirements Engineering. This section provides an overview of the most pertinent works. Notably, the issue of third-party tool selection has been addressed across different research streams, such as Third-Party Tools for RE and COTS Selection and Procurement in RE.

The analysis of the DESMET project underscores the importance of case studies for objectively improving internal processes. The focus on objective improvement and the integration of precise schemas could thus constitute a fundamental element for the development of a new evaluation approach [6]. We adhere to this recommendation by centralizing our approach around pilots. The work of Maiden and Ncube emphasizes the significance of detailed requirements and the presence of stakeholder representatives during product evaluation. This highlights the critical role of requirement details and stakeholder involvement in a comprehensive evaluation process. They provide a very interesting approach in a possible requirement elicitation process step; however, they lack an integrated systematic approach for evaluating the fulfillment of the elicited requirements [7].

Furthermore, Briand's work - COTS Evaluation and Selection - emphasizes the importance of qualitative criteria, software prototypes, and stakeholder representatives, similar to Maiden and Ncube [7], during COTS selection. These factors stress that quantitative criteria alone are insufficient, and qualitative aspects must be taken into account [8]. Another foundation is Matulevicius's structured evaluation framework. This framework emphasizes the benefits of evaluating RE tools based on their individual strengths. Implementing the individual strengths of a tool thus provides a differentiated perspective that challenges the general assumption of a "One-Size-Fits-All" approach. According to his work, a flexibly adaptable approach could lead to success in specific cases [9].

In addition to the general development of an evaluation process, Gotel and Mäder highlight the discrepancy in organizational understanding, leading to disparities between the benefits and implementation efforts of third-party tools.

This insight underscores the need to consider the actual benefits of a tool in relation to implementation costs [10]. To develop an approach that remains applicable in the future, Mohamed, Ruhe, and Eberlein's work [11] addresses the identified research gaps in the selection of commercial software components. One of these gaps highlights the constant need to develop adaptable selection methods to changing requirements, ensuring that these methods do not disregard current requirements in a rapidly evolving IT landscape after just a few months [11]. In a comprehensive evaluation approach, all these insights could converge to develop an approach that considers precise schemas, individual strength assessment, detailed requirements, qualitative criteria, and continuous adaptation. Furthermore, one of the identified research gaps in the discussed studies is the lack of adaptability in prioritizing requirements. Also the IREB handbook, one of the standards for RE, includes a section about RE tool evaluation. They give many hints what to consider for a RE tool assessment (e.g. explicitly mention all relevant stakeholders for this scenario), but they don't describe different steps of the assessment process (e.g. MoScow) and give less guidance [12].

Regarding Munich Re, the adoption of this hybrid approach stems from the firm conviction that a higher quality of requirements engineering directly correlates with an improved software product. The modeling of requirements stands out as a crucial phase within the software development lifecycle.

2.2   State of the Practice

Previous to this work, when Munich Re evaluated third-party tools, they only standardized risk assessment, but not the actual requirements engineering and assessment process. Therefore, when an employee wanted to integrate a potential tool into a software development project, this was done based on self-perceived criteria. Often, suitability for the current project was considered as primary criterion, with little attention to a broader, project-spanning evaluation. This often lead to focus on RE tool requirements only fit to the current situation. To overcome these limitations, the approach presented here attempts to implement a structured methodology for the objective assessment of the suitability of a third-party tool. According to our experience from consulting other companies globally, this is not a Munich Re specific problem, but instead a common approach which, according to our subjective observations, leads to two problems: First, the selection is too often based on good marketing, charismatic salesmen and fancy power points instead of objective criteria. Second, it can lead to a tool landscape which is difficult to govern by the company's IT management.

2.3   Research Gap

The analysis of existing research literature regarding an approach to evaluate third-party products reveals several previously unaddressed gaps. Matulevicius focuses specifically on the individual strengths of a tool but downplays the need for a flexibly adaptable prioritization, leading to an unclear consideration of prioritization mechanisms. Matulevicius, Gotel, Mäder, and Briand also indicate consideration of a variety of requirement categories. However, they seem to restrict tool evaluations to a limited number of requirement categories, overlooking the importance ranking of each category and adaptability of approaches for future and evolving relevant requirement categories. Gotel and Mäder highlight disparities between expected benefits and implementation efforts, but fail to provide objective measurement criteria for a preselection of suitability for potential implementation-lack of measurable criteria development. Maiden, Ncube, and Briand underscore stakeholder integration, yet the appropriate inclusion of all relevant stakeholder requirements remains unclear-a deficiency in stakeholder requirements analysis. Accordingly, our approach aims to integrate those ideas into an effective approach for selecting a third-party products. The approach needs to integrate adaptable prioritization, expandable category coverage, measurable criteria, and stakeholder inclusion.

3   C1: Third Party Tool Selection (TPTS) Process

The evaluation process presented below distinguishes itself through the integration of established methods, including comprehensive requirement gathering, conducting proprietary studies, categorizing, and involving users in the requirements. What sets it apart is its innovative approach to addressing gaps by incorporating adaptable prioritization, expandable categories, measurable criteria, and enhanced stakeholder involvement. The process thus tackles weaknesses in previous approaches. This section elaborates on the structure and implementation of this approach, which not only builds upon prior research but also actively contributes to closing existing gaps (Fig. 1).

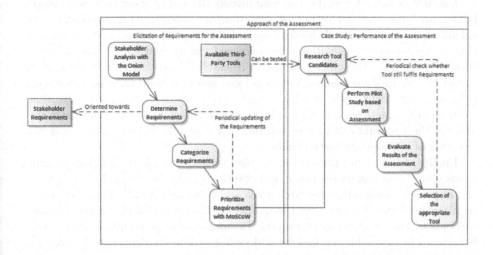

Fig. 1. The individual steps of the TPTS process.

Step-by-Step Process:

1. **Stakeholder Analysis with the Onion Model:** Identify and analyze stakeholders' needs using the onion model, providing a comprehensive understanding of their requirements [13].
2. **Determine Requirements Aligned with Stakeholder Needs:** Derive requirements based on the stakeholder analysis to ensure alignment with their needs and expectations [12].
3. **Categorize Requirements:** Organize and categorize the requirements for clarity and better management.
4. **Prioritize Requirements using the MoSCoW Method:** Prioritize requirements using the MoSCoW method, regularly updating this prioritization in line with evolving needs [14].
5. **Perform Pilot Study for Tool Assessment:** Conduct a comprehensive study to assess and test various third-party tools that could potentially meet the established requirements.
6. **Evaluate Results of Assessments:** Analyze and evaluate the outcomes of the assessments conducted on the selected tools.
7. **Selection of the Appropriate Tool:** Periodically assess if the selected tool continues to meet the evolving requirements and choose the most appropriate tool accordingly.

Using these eight steps, a structured methodology is intended to be implemented for a possible advancement of the current state of research. Similarly, this methodology could address the research gaps identified in the related works. Lack of prioritization, a limited number of categories, insufficient measurability and objectivity, a narrow focus on modeling, and a deficiency in considering all stakeholders.

Initially, a solid foundation is established through a comprehensive stakeholder analysis and derivation of requirements, allowing for a holistic consideration of relevant stakeholders and their specific needs. The categorization of requirements contributes to increased clarity and easier management, thereby enhancing the efficiency of the research. Moreover, the application of the MoSCoW method ensures a clear prioritization of requirements, facilitating a focused alignment with essential aspects and optimizing resource utilization. Additionally, practical case studies for tool assessment provide a realistic evaluation of the suitability of various solutions for research objectives, aiding in the selection of appropriate instruments.

Finally, and equally important, regular review and adaptation to changing needs secure continuous relevance and effectiveness in the research. This proactive approach ensures that research goals and tools remain in line with dynamic requirements, thus maintaining the quality and relevance of the empirical work throughout the entire research process. In summary, these steps offer a comprehensive and sustainable method for addressing various challenges in the creation of assessments for third-party products.

4   C2: Feasibility Study: Selection of a Requirements Modelling Tool at Munich Re

This section reports on the application of the process described in the previous section onto the selection of a requirements modelling tool at Munich Re. For this, we first explain the study design. We then report the results by explaining the outcome for each of the steps of the TPTS process before summarizing and discussing these results, including their validity. As much as possible in industrial contexts, we support the ideas of open science. We therefore decided to publish an anonymized version of the dataset at [15].

4.1   Study Design

Context Munich Re: Munich Re Group is one of the world's leading risk carriers with more than 140 years of unrivalled risk-related expertise. The group covers the entire value chain of reinsurance, primary insurance, insurance related services and capital market solutions with 40.000+ employees and a global presence in 50+ countries. Driving the digital transformation of the insurance industry in order to push forward the boundaries of insurability and providing coverage for extraordinary risks such as rocket launches, renewable energies or cyberattacks are the main goals next to addressing and insuring climate risks to make the world more resilient.

For their insurance business, they develop and maintain a variety of individual software systems. Since the produced systems often involve many stakeholders across the globe, and software systems are often run by changing, distributed teams over a long period of time, good requirements engineering (RE) and RE artifacts are essential to the company.

Requirements Modelling Tools. At Munich Re, there are two different approaches to creating diagrams: that of the 'Modeller' and the 'Drawer'. The 'Modeller' is a user who reuses elements across different diagrams. This means they reuse already created and defined elements, such as classes, objects, or relationships, in various diagrams. In contrast, the 'Drawer' creates entirely new elements from scratch for each new diagram, focusing more on short term usability than long term consistency.

4.2   Results

In the following we guide through the results of each individual step of the TPTS process.

Step 1: Stakeholder Analysis with the Onion Model: In the stakeholder analysis using the Onion Model, the following stakeholders have been identified. As components of the Business System, the stakeholders encompass the *Business Analyst, Solution Architect, Application Developer*, and the *Software Provider*. Solely the *external consultant* is found as part of the Integrative System. In the External Environment, the stakeholders comprise *Shareholders*, *Clients/Customers*, *Regulatory Authorities*, and *competitors*.

Step 2: Determine Requirements Aligned with Stakeholder Needs: In the following, we conducted elicitation sessions with experienced Requirements Engineers from Munich Re, engaging in exchanges on potential requirements over several weeks. Additionally, based on these discussions, we analyzed a handful of internal documents to advance the requirements gathering process. This lead to a total of seventy-four identified requirements, including ten explicit requirements from regulatory authorities, such as 'Availability of Access Control and User Roles/Groups'. Fifty-seven of all requirements are gathered from potential users within the innermost circle of the Business System, as they constitute the end users of the product. The individual requirements span from 'Import of Data' and 'Collaboration among multiple users' to 'Availability to create a link to a specific document' and 'Availability of API for database'. The remaining seven requirements are distributed among other stakeholders. A detailed list of requirements can be found in [15]. In this study, we frequently employ the term 'requirements' to emphasize the diversity of demands that extend beyond purely functional considerations. It is crucial to note that, in line with the arguments presented by Glinz, we predominantly use the term 'Soft Requirements' to articulate such demands. In contrast to the conventional distinction between functional and non-functional requirements, the term 'Soft Requirements' encompasses a broader spectrum of demands that may include both qualitative and quantitative aspects. The key differentiator lies in the gradationally measurable fulfillment, enabling 'Soft Requirements' to facilitate a more flexible characterization of system demands. [16] Ultimately, throughout this work, the requirements are intended to be assessed as either fulfilled or not fulfilled.

Step 3: Categorize Requirements: Since the preceding step of this approach only provided an unordered list of requirements, this step aims to categorize all requirements in a structured manner. The categories are subdivided into identified core competencies that a third-party tool should be able to implement. An additional category stems from the field of modeling, which is crucial for the practical case of Munich Re but might not be relevant in a different scenario. Consequently, the following eight overarching categories have emerged, each having its own category-specific subcategories, as detailed in Table 2.

Step 4: Prioritize Requirements using the MoSCoW Method: Prioritization of requirements has been conducted using the MoSCoW method. In this process, all identified requirements have been assessed using the MoSCoW method. Security requirements, primarily stemming from the fulfillment of security agency criteria, have been categorized as 'Must' criteria. Specifically, in this case, exactly 15 requirements have been designated as 'Must'. 34 requirements essential for modeling at Munich Re, such as modeling with UML and element reusability, are rated as 'Should'. Similarly, requirements for data and model documentation, as well as the creation and reuse of templates for model export, fall under this 'Should' category. In contrast, needs with potential workarounds are classified as 'Could', comprising a total of 25 requirements. For example, the requirement for 'Flexibility in using custom functions' falls into this category. To achieve significant results in prioritization, regular updates to this prioritization were necessary, adapting to the continually evolving project needs and context understanding.

Step 5: Research Tool Candidates: For the shortlist, we opportunistically selected three representative tools, as a detailed examination of all tools available on the market would exceed the scope of this paper. This selection is based on the observation that various tools have been utilized in the RE-process of the software development lifecycle, driven by the individual preferences of different team members. There is now a concerted effort to reach a consensus on a unified tool within the framework of this lifecycle (Table 1).

Table 1. Shortlist of all Tools considered

Tool	Manufacturer	URL	Drawing/ Modeling
Enterprise Architect	Sparx Systems	https://sparxsystems.com	Modeling
Miro	Miro	https://miro.com	Drawing
Draw.IO	JGraph Ltd und draw.io AG	https://www.drawio.com	Drawing

Step 6: Perform Pilot Study for Tool Assessment: After categorizing and classifying the requirements of all stakeholders, we executed a pilot for each potential tool in this step. The objective is to determine whether and to what extent a tool can fulfill all the requirements of a third-party tool, independent from marketing slides or website promises. Only when each potential tool has completed this process, we can establish a meaningful result. In this paper, we test the Enterprise Architect, Miro, and Draw.IO. These tools were either already licensed at Munich Re or, in the case of Draw.IO, can be tested and evaluated for free. When conducting this process, a requirement is considered fulfilled when it meets the precise criteria specified in its formulation. A 'yes' in this context signifies that the requirement has been successfully fulfilled. The approach of categorizing a requirement as either fulfilled or not fulfilled compels the user to articulate the requirement clearly and aims to eliminate any room for interpretation.

Step 7: Evaluate Results of Assessments: Analyze and evaluate the outcomes of the assessments conducted on the selected tools. In cases where none of the tools achieves 100 percent for the 'Must' category, it is crucial to recognize that the suitability of a tool necessitates an absolute fulfillment of 'Must' requirements. These requirements are indispensable for effective integration and utilization of a third-party tool.

Table 2. Third-party assessment results for Enterprise Architect, percentage of fulfillment discriminated by priority according to MoSCoW

Category	Must	Should	Could
Functionality	100%	67%	100%
Ease of Use	100%	75%	100%
Customizability	N/A	N/A	83%
Integration	100%	N/A	100%
Collaboration	100%	100%	60%
Security	100%	100%	100%
Support	N/A	75%	50%
Performance	100%	67%	100%
Total results	**100%**	**83%**	**85%**

Analyzing the percentage fulfillment of the Enterprise Architect during the conducted pilot study, as depicted in the Table 2, it is evident that the tool successfully satisfied all essential criteria. In the aggregate, the Enterprise Architect demonstrated the highest degree of compliance, surpassing other third-party tools considered in the study (Table 3).

Table 3. Third-party assessment results for Miro, percentage of fulfillment discriminated by priority according to MoSCoW

Category	Must	Should	Could
Functionality	100%	33%	40%
Ease of Use	100%	100%	100%
Customizability	N/A	N/A	17%
Integration	100%	N/A	100%
Collaboration	100%	71%	80%
Security	100%	100%	100%
Support	N/A	100%	100%
Performance	100%	100%	100%
Total results	**100%**	**83%**	**65%**

Miro, as an external work platform, facilitates collaborative workspaces and impresses with its comprehensive yet straightforward design. The intuitively organized user interface allows for immediate tool engagement. The restricted quantity of icons, although beneficial for usability, signifies limitations in the tool's customization capabilities, offering a finite range of functions and scripting options. While Miro excels in initiating diagram creation, it reveals constraints in accommodating expert-defined functionalities specified in requirements, necessitating a more intricate modeling environment (Table 4).

Table 4. Third-party assessment results for Draw.IO, percentage of fulfillment discriminated by priority according to MoSCoW

Category	Must	Should	Could
Functionality	75%	0	20%
Ease of Use	100%	100%	100%
Customizability	N/A	N/A	0%
Integration	100%	N/A	50%
Collaboration	100%	43%	40%
Security	25%	0%	0%
Support	N/A	100%	0%
Performance	100%	67%	100%
Total results	**73%**	**52%**	**31%**

The apparent results of the analysis initially suggest that Draw.IO is not suitable for modeling. However, the fundamental capacity to generate accurate UML diagrams and the potential integration with the Azure environment, alongside robust support and integration features such as Azure icons, prove notably advantageous. Nevertheless, the tool's security measures exhibit significant deficiencies. The tool lacks mechanisms to ascertain document access, revision tracking, or prevent unauthorized modifications or deletions within the entire system.

Step 8: Selection of the Appropriate Tool: In the final step of the approach, the conducted case studies are compared based on the results of each individual tool. The essential indicator of a tool's suitability is the degree of fulfillment of the requirements prioritized using the MoSCoW method. It is important to note that periodic assessments are necessary to determine whether the chosen tool continues to align with the continuously evolving requirements (Table 5).

Comparing tools, Draw.IO consistently falls short by at least 25 percent across prioritization levels, rendering it unsuitable for Munich Re's documentation of functional requirements as part of the product documentation. Although proficient in diagram creation and syntax adherence, it doesn't meet Munich Re's stringent security standards when combined with Visual Studio Code. As a result, only Enterprise Architect and Miro remain viable for Munich Re, excelling

Table 5. Comparative Assessment of the three Tools based on their individual Results

Category	Enterprise Architect	Miro	Draw.IO
Must	100%	100%	73%
Should	83%	83%	52%
Could	85%	65%	31%
Won't	not present	in this	study
Price of the Tool	Individual costs	Individual costs	Free of charge

in different categories crucial for project success. Enterprise Architect comprehensively meets stakeholder requirements but can enhance "Usability" and "Collaboration," whereas Miro excels in fostering collaborative environments. Both tools offer adaptable pricing, eliminating significant cost differentials for tool evaluation. Strategic investment in appropriate tools is vital for optimal performance, espacially given Munich Re's size.

In summary, Enterprise Architect emerges as the most fitting tool for Munich Re, facilitating element reuse, streamlining documentation, and preventing future project misconceptions in business analysis.

4.3   Discussion

The implementation of this Third Party Tool Selection (TPTS) process as an effective decision-making process for a third-party tool requires an advancement of existing approaches. We attempt to address initially identified gaps, such as lack of adaptability, incorporation of qualitative aspects, and the categorization and prioritization of requirements, through a eight-step process.

Initiating with the Stakeholder Analysis using the Onion Model, the approach provides a precise foundation to understand stakeholder needs, classified by their importance. This initial step allows for the derivation of detailed requirements supporting stakeholder expectations. During requirement elicitation, particular emphasis is placed on achieving a balance between the objectivity and adaptability of the requirements. However, as we explained earlier, we mostly used what are known as 'soft requirements'. While we were working, it was difficult to say exactly when these requirements were met and when they were not. Basically, these requirements are about personal opinions and are not easy to put into categories like 'met' and 'not met'.

Subsequently, the categorization of requirements facilitates management and enhances clarity in the later evaluation of the process. Prioritization using the MoSCoW method is a dynamic step allowing for regular updates of priorities. However, a potential feasibility issue arises, considering the significant additional effort required for continuous evaluations. Thus, in practical application, this step might infrequently be updated, relying on prior assumptions. The incorporation of case studies for each tool evaluation provides the advantage of elucidating individual strengths. It is imperative for the user to be aware that a potentially time-consuming process precedes the implementation.

The evaluation of results, based on the percentage fulfillment of MoSCoW categories, plays a central role in decision-making. The subjective nature of potential implementation is evident. When comparing multiple tools using this approach, as in the case of Munich Re, it is evident that the Enterprise Architect performs the best. However, there is no clear threshold indicating the suitability of a tool based on the fulfillment percentage. This introduces a potential discrepancy regarding whether the process is only applicable in a comparative context or if the process should establish a certain threshold for percentage fulfillment. The implementation may potentially depend on the knowledge and experience of individual methods. In this case, the execution was carried out without strictly necessary expert knowledge, indicating that fundamental knowledge is sufficient. For future research, there is the possibility to examine the potential impacts of the required expertise.

In addition, the methods presented are based on successful applications at Munich Re. This positive experience underlines the relevance of the proposed selection process for third-party tools. There is an opportunity for future research to share individual methods and validate them in various corporate settings. This could lead to further refinement of the process to improve applicability and effectiveness. Nevertheless, this study demonstrates the practicality of the approach, while highlighting the need to expand the scope of research in future studies.

Lastly, the periodic execution of evaluations constitutes an essential part of the process. Although this approach consistently identifies the optimally performing tool for a given case, resource considerations and feasibility play a crucial role.

In conclusion, we provided a systematic approach, for which our study showed the feasibility for Munich Re. According to our subjective, personal impression, we would also argue that the approach is more efficient and effective than approaches previously applied at Munich Re. However, a systematic analysis with objective, measurable results for this claim is both methodologically challenging and requires a fitting opportunity for an upcoming tool selection case and tremendous management support in the company. Until this opportunity arrives, this analysis remains future work. The following section will discuss to which extent the process provides objective results (see *internal validity*).'

Threats to Validity The goal of the presented study is to show feasibility of the proposed process. Threats to validity exist with regard to both internal as well as external validity.

Internal validity: In the execution of an assessment for a third-party tool at Munich Re, a significant risk lies in the potential subjectivity of requirements identified and derived during stakeholder analysis. This subjectivity may be rooted in individual interpretations and opinions of stakeholders, leading to a distortion of actual needs and, consequently, compromising the internal validity of the entire assessment. A plausible risk pertains to the incorrect allocation of requirements during the organization and categorization process. Incorrect assignments may result in a flawed interpretation of requirements, subsequently leading to inaccurate conclusions in the evaluation of tools. Another threat to internal validity arises from the clear fulfillment or non-fulfillment of requirements being determined by a third-party tool, yet lacking an explicit method for measuring these results. Furthermore, a threat to internal validity exists in the possibility of neglecting periodic reviews of the selected tools, requirements, and prioritization. This omission could render the results outdated over time, with changes in requirements going unnoticed, thus jeopardizing the relevance and validity of the findings. We tried to address all of these needs through researcher triangulation and majority voting. However, these threats remain present as it is not uncommon in such in-vivo studies.

External validity: Since the TPTS process does not depends on Munich Re or even the insurance domain, we would argue that the findings generalize beyond the presented case. However, C2 only provides a single-case, single-context study according to the terminology by Yin [17] and provides therefore only limited evidence for generalizability. Accordingly, future work needs to expand this work to more cases within the context (i.e. more third party tool selections) and more contexts beyond Munich Re. This will indicate which project factors required additional adaptations to the process.

5   Summary and Outlook

The paper addresses the challenge of efficiently selecting third-party software solutions in companies. The proposed Third Party Tool Selection (TPTS) process is combining existing approaches, consisting of eight steps, including stakeholder analysis, requirement elicitation, categorization, prioritization, research of tool candidates, conducting a pilot study, evaluating the results, and selecting the appropriate tool. The proposed approach has been validated through a feasibility study at Munich Re, confirming its suitability, yet only for this case. Therefore, practitioners are encouraged to integrate and advance the method in their own decision-making processes for third-party tools.

One insight of this work emphasizes the need for regular assessments but highlights potential practicality issues due to high resource utilization. The subjective nature of stakeholder requirement elicitation and the absence of a clear threshold value for determining tool suitability are also challenging. Internal validity risks primarily lie in the subjectivity of stakeholder analysis, possible incorrect assignment of requirements, and overlooked verifications. External validity is considered limited, and future work should extend the approach to multiple cases and contexts. The feasibility of the approach has been successfully demonstrated through the pilot study with Munich Re, and future efforts will focus on efficiency and effectiveness. Transferability to other projects and companies is sought, with the aim of identifying future procurement decisions similar to the previous ones, enabling a comparison of effort and results. This could lead to collaboration with other companies and researchers for the further development and validation of the TPTS process.

References

1. Jurison, J.: The role of risk and return in information technology outsourcing decisions. In: Risk Management, pp. 95–103. Routledge (2019)
2. Ghodeswar, B., Vaidyanathan, J.: Business process outsourcing: an approach to gain access to world-class capabilities. Bus. Process Manage. J. **14**(1), 23–38 (2008)
3. Dhar, S., Balakrishnan, B.: Risks, benefits, and challenges in global IT outsourcing: perspectives and practices. J. Global Inf. Manage. (JGIM) **14**(3), 59–89 (2006)
4. Lacity, M., Burgess, A.: and Leslie Willcocks. Risk and Opportunity. A&C Black, The Rise of Legal Services Outsourcing (2014)
5. Statista. Rückversicherung: Statista-Dossier zur Branche der Rückversicherer. Hamburg: Statista (2019)
6. Kitchenham, B., Pickard, L., Pfleeger, S.L.: Case studies for method and tool evaluation. IEEE Softw. **12**(4), 52–62 (1995)
7. Maiden, N.A., Ncube, C.: Acquiring COTS software selection requirements. IEEE Softw. **15**(2), 46–56 (1998)
8. Briand, L.C.: COTS evaluation and selection. In: Proceedings of International Conference on Software Maintenance (Cat. No. 98CB36272), pp. 222–223. IEEE (1998)
9. Raimundas Matulevičius. Process support for requirements engineering: a requirements engineering tool evaluation approach. University of Tartu (2005)
10. Gotel, O., Mader, P.: How to select a requirements management tool: initial steps. In: Proceedings of 17th IEEE International Requirements Engineering Conference, pp. 365–367. IEEE (2009)
11. Mohamed, A., Ruhe, G., Eberlein, A.: COTS selection: past, present, and future. In: 14th Annual IEEE International Conference and Workshops on the Engineering of Computer-Based Systems (ECBS 2007), pp. 103–114. IEEE (2007)
12. Glinz, M., et al.: Handbook for the CPRE foundation level according to the IREB Standard. In: International Requirements Engineering Board (2022)
13. Alexander, I., Robertson, S.: Understanding project sociology by modeling stakeholders. IEEE Softw. **21**(1), 23–27 (2004)
14. Kravchenko, T., Bogdanova, T., Shevgunov, T.: Ranking requirements using MoSCoW methodology in practice. In: Silhavy, R. (ed.) Cybernetics Perspectives in Systems: Proceedings of 11th Computer Science On-line Conference 2022. LNNS, vol. 3, pp. 188–199. Springer, Cham (2022) https://doi.org/10.1007/978-3-031-09073-8_18
15. Koschinsky, M., Femmer, H., Schindler, C.: Dataset from the paper "a process proposal for requirements engineering for third-party products and a preliminary evaluation at Munich Re", January 2024. https://doi.org/10.6084/m9.figshare.24749637, https://figshare.com/articles/dataset/Dataset_from_the_Paper_A_Process_Proposal_for_Requirements_Engineering_for_Third-Party_Products_and_a_Preliminary_Evaluation_at_Munich_Re_/24749637/1
16. Glinz, M.: On non-functional requirements. In: 15th IEEE International Requirements Engineering Conference (RE 2007), pp. 21–26. IEEE (2007)
17. Yin, R.K.: Case Study Research: Design and Methods, vol. 5. Sage, Thousand Oaks (2009)

Software Quality

Source Code Clone Detection Using Unsupervised Similarity Measures

Jorge Martinez-Gil$^{(\boxtimes)}$ (iD)

Software Competence Center Hagenberg GmbH,
Softwarepark 32a, 4232 Hagenberg, Austria
`jorge.martinez-gil@scch.at`

Abstract. Assessing similarity in source code has gained significant attention in recent years due to its importance in software engineering tasks such as clone detection and code search and recommendation. This work presents a comparative analysis of unsupervised similarity measures for identifying source code clone detection. The goal is to overview the current state-of-the-art techniques, their strengths, and weaknesses. To do that, we compile the existing unsupervised strategies and evaluate their performance on a benchmark dataset to guide software engineers in selecting appropriate methods for their specific use cases. The source code of this study is available at https://github.com/jorge-martinez-gil/codesim

Keywords: Software Engineering · Clone Detection · Similarity Measures · Code Similarity

1 Introduction

Source code clone detection holds increasing importance in the current software engineering landscape, and its significance is likely to grow even further [1]. The reason is that this approach is crucial in software development since it can help address various problems during software maintenance [18]. Clones are duplicate or similar pieces of code within a software project. Therefore, consider the chaotic situation that would happen if a bug is fixed or a change is made to a piece of code but not to its duplicates. To avoid such situations, developers should have tools to automatically evaluate the likeness between code fragments based on various aspects of their form and functionality [33,34].

In this work, we address this challenge from the point of view of using similarity measures, which are generally used for textual comparisons. When working with general and source code similarity, it is necessary to distinguish between supervised and unsupervised approaches [26]. On the one hand, supervised approaches require a training set of pairs of code fragments labeled as similar or dissimilar, which is often difficult to get, at least in terms of the necessary volume. On the other hand, unsupervised approaches do not require a training set, and they can be used to measure the similarity of any two code

© The Author(s), under exclusive license to Springer Nature Switzerland AG 2024
P. Bludau et al. (Eds.): SWQD 2024, LNBIP 505, pp. 21–37, 2024.
https://doi.org/10.1007/978-3-031-56281-5_2

fragments with no prior knowledge and a low consumption of computational resources.

This work evaluates at least one representative implementation of unsupervised similarity measures. In this regard, we explore measures ranging from trivial strategies for token comparison to the more advanced comparison of embeddings [31]. To facilitate a thorough assessment, we use a benchmark dataset comprising diverse code fragments with varying degrees of similarity and check the performance of each similarity measure across the dataset.

Our analysis focuses on shedding light on practical applicability and efficiency. The rationale behind summarizing the existing body of knowledge and identifying research gaps is to offer a resource for software engineers interested in unsupervised measures for detecting source code clones. Furthermore, in contrast to recent works, which address the challenge from a purely qualitative perspective, our work aims at a quantitative analysis, with an empirical analysis of all the methods considered.

Therefore, this work's primary and overall contribution aims to guide the choice of appropriate unsupervised similarity measures for clone detection. Additionally, it identifies promising directions for future research in source code similarity assessment. The following specific contributions achieve this:

- We present the fundamental challenge regarding clone detection and the possibility of building solutions to cope with the absence of labeled data and different coding styles.
- We compile an extensive collection of unsupervised semantic similarity measures, being able to compare textual information to elucidate the most promising measures in this context.
- We empirically evaluate this collection of unsupervised measures focusing on accuracy, time consumption, practical feasibility, and other metrics such as precision, recall, and f-measures. Our results indicate that several measures could be valid source code clone detection tools.

The remainder of this paper is structured as follows: Sect. 2 introduces the background of this critical challenge of code clone detection. Section 3 technically explains the similarity measures that we are using to face this challenge and shows several examples. Section 4 evaluates all the similarity measures reviewed in the previous version using a complete benchmark dataset. Section 5 discusses the results of our experiments. Finally, the paper concludes with lessons learned and lines of future work.

2   Background

This section presents the information necessary to understand the challenge. First, we define code similarity assessment; second, we explain why this challenge is so significant nowadays; and third, we describe the implications and impact of the challenge in academia and industry.

2.1   Problem Definition

It seems clear that code duplication can lead to inconsistencies, especially if a change is made in one part of the code but not in its clones [29]. In this context, it is also important to differentiate between code similarity measurement and identification of source code clones. Code similarity measurement is a broad concept, and clone identification is one of its applications. For instance, the most similar instances can be reported as cloned instances just using a threshold value to filter out the results of code similarity measurement [4].

Although there is no strict definition for the assessment of code similarity, it is possible to describe the problem formally, such as given a set of code fragments $S = \{C_1, C_2, \ldots, C_n\}$, the goal is to find a function $f : S \times S \rightarrow [0,1]$ that computes the similarity score between any C_i and C_j.

Therefore, f should map a given pair (C_i, C_j) to a value in the continuous interval $[0,1]$, whereby:

- $f(C_i, C_j) = 0$ indicates that C_i and C_j are completely dissimilar
- $f(C_i, C_j) = 1$ indicates that C_i and C_j are identical
- $f(C_i, C_j)$ increases as the similarity between C_i and C_j increases and vice versa

The function f should compare C_i and C_j, considering various characteristics such as variables, constants, function calls, comments, overall logic, or any other code element susceptible to being compared [35]. Then, clone detection can be implemented to discriminate between instances using, for example, a point value separating clones and non-clones. Furthermore, although it was not considered in the frame of this work, it would be desirable that the results could be accompanied by an explanation [20] for facilitating human assessment.

Similarity Categories. Multiple copies of similar code throughout a software project can make managing the codebase difficult. However, not all the cases are equal. In comparing pieces of code, some recent literature has categorized the code similarities into four categories [3]. These categories help us understand the degree of resemblance between two code fragments so that each category represents a different level of likeness:

- Category I: The code fragments are identical, with just minor variations in white spaces and annotations.
- Category II: The code fragments have the same structure, but there are differences in the names of the identifiers, data types, spaces, and comments.
- Category III: Additionally, parts of the code might be removed or altered, or new parts could be incorporated.
- Category IV: The code fragments may appear different but implement analogous functionality.

The rationale behind this categorization is to provide insights into code comparison and help software engineers understand the cases they must face to make better-informed decisions. However, more datasets with this categorization are needed, since the existing ones do not usually differentiate.

2.2 The Importance of Unsupervised Measures

Detecting code clones is essential for maintaining software quality [16]. Unsupervised code similarity assessment can help address this challenge since several practical aspects are common to many software development projects:

- Unsupervised measures do not rely on labeled training data, making use of a ground truth unnecessary. Labeled examples are only needed to validate the performance of unsupervised approaches.
- Code can be written in various programming languages, using different coding styles, etc. Some unsupervised measures can accommodate this variety without a complex universal similarity metric.
- Understanding the meaning of code is complicated because code fragments may be functionally equivalent even if they look dissimilar, and vice versa. Some unsupervised measures can face that challenge.
- Codebases often contain comments, noise, etc. Some unsupervised measures can differentiate between meaningful code patterns and unrelated elements.

2.3 Future Perspectives

Duplicate code increases the maintenance burden because changes must be replicated across all clones, which is time-consuming and error-prone [5]. Therefore, identifying and refactoring these clones can reduce the maintenance effort [11].

Nowadays, where many open-source libraries and code repositories exist, unsupervised source code similarity measurement can be helpful; it enables developers to navigate this diverse ecosystem and search for relevant code efficiently with low consumption of computational resources [27]. This importance extends to facilitating code reuse, which is crucial for reducing development time in the face of growing software complexity [9].

Furthermore, detecting code similarities can improve security by identifying vulnerabilities with known code patterns in the context of growing security troubles. It can also contribute to code maintainability and refactoring efforts, allowing developers to ensure software projects' long-term sustainability.

We can also think of applications within various industries that benefit from increased compliance and reliability in critical systems. Furthermore, collaboration tools facilitate cooperation by connecting developers with similar code, and quality assurance strategies could benefit from unsupervised code similarity measurement by identifying similar cases for complete test coverage.

3 Methods

Early approaches for assessing the similarity relied on just textual analysis [25]. These techniques, while efficient, often struggle to capture the structural aspects of code, resulting in limited accuracy [12]. However, the field has evolved a lot in recent years. More sophisticated similarity measures assumed to perform better have been proposed [10].

3.1 Unsupervised Methods

There are many methods (a.k.a. semantic similarity measures) to determine the similarity between textual entities. Each measure offers a unique approach based on specific characteristics or representations of the compared entities. From the literature, we have identified about 21 families that could be applied here, briefly explained below in alphabetical order.

- **Abstract Syntax Trees (ASTs) Similarity**: ASTs are hierarchical representations of the structure of code. AST similarity measures compare the structural similarity between different AST representing code [22].
- **Bag-of-Words Similarity**: This similarity measure calculates the resemblance between texts by considering the frequency of individual words in each text without considering word order or structure [7].
- **Code Embeddings Similarity (CodeBERT)**: Code embeddings are vector representations of source code. This method measures the similarity of code based on these embeddings [2]. Please note that we use them here without recalibration.
- **Comments Similarity**: It measures the similarity between code comments, which can be helpful for code documentation and understanding. In principle, many traditional text similarity measures can be used [28].
- **Fuzzy Matching Similarity**: Fuzzy matching compares strings for minor syntactical variations. It is often used in data matching and search applications [37], but we apply it here to measure code similarity.
- **Function Calls Similarity**: This family measures the similarity between different code fragments based on the functions and procedures in the code fragments [39].
- **Graph-based Similarity**: It calculates similarity based on a graph's relations, which could represent various data structures and dependencies [40].
- **Jaccard Similarity**: Jaccard similarity measures the similarity between sets of tokens by comparing their intersection and union. It is commonly used in text analysis, recommendation systems, and information retrieval [14].
- **Levenshtein Similarity**: This measure, also known as edit distance, calculates the similarity between two strings by measuring the number of edits needed to transform one into the other [24].
- **Longest Common Subsequence (LCS) Similarity**: LCS similarity calculates the similarity between two sequences by finding the longest common subsequence between them [6].
- **Metrics Similarity**: The idea is first to compute various metrics related to the source code and then estimate the similarity between the values obtained [30]. We are using here: code length, cyclomatic complexity, number of variables, etc.
- **N-grams Similarity**: N-grams are contiguous sequences of 'n' items (e.g., words or characters). N-gram similarity measures the similarity between texts based on shared n-grams [8].

- **Output Analysis Similarity**: This method measures the similarity of program outputs, which can be helpful for testing and debugging. In principle, and if we assume the outputs as text, a wide range of traditional text similarity measures can be used [28].
- **Perceptual Hashing Similarity**: Perceptual hashing, often used in image similarity, aims to generate a fixed-length hash code from images. In our context, this method measures similarity based on hashes from visual representation of the code [32].
- **Program Dependence Graph Similarity**: This measure assesses the similarity between code by analyzing the program dependence graph, which represents the dependencies between program elements [23]. It is different from the Graph-based method since focuses on control dependencies.
- **Rolling Hash Similarity**: A rolling hash is a hash function that can be updated efficiently as new data is processed. Rolling hash similarity can compare substrings (hashes) in large texts [15]. We use here for comparing code.
- **Running-Karp-Rabin Greedy-String-Tiling (RKR-GST) Similarity**: It is often used in the context of detecting plagiarism by identifying maximal sequences of contiguous matching tokens (tiles) [38].
- **Semdiff Similarity**: Semdiff is a method for detecting semantic differences between program versions. Semdiff similarity measures how code changes affect the program's semantics [17].
- **Semantic Clone Similarity**: This method family tries to measure the similarity of code fragments based on the semantic meaning of the names of the program elements (variables, methods, etc.) [13].
- **TF-IDF Similarity**: Term Frequency-Inverse Document Frequency (TF-IDF) is used in text analysis to measure the importance of words in a text compared to a larger corpus. TF-IDF similarity compares texts based on these weighted terms [19].
- **Winnow Similarity**: It is a text comparison algorithm that identifies similar texts by hashing them and comparing their fingerprints [36].

Next, we will look at some Java code examples, representing some interesting cases of source code cloning, illustrating how all these similarity measures quantify code similarity in practice.

3.2   Examples

In the examples below, *T1* and *T01* are two Java classes that produce the same output but with different approaches: *T1* prints the statement *Welcome to Java* five times using five separate print statements. *T01* achieves the same output using a for loop that iterates five times, printing the statement on each iteration. From the perspective of code clone detection, these two classes are Category IV clones. The reason is that both are pieces of code that perform the same operations but are implemented through different syntactic variations.

Even though the actual text of the code differs, the for loop versus repeated print statements, the meaning, and the output are the same. However, detecting such code clones can be challenging because it is not just a matter of matching text strings but requires a deep understanding of the code's logic. However, it is common to find similar cases in real settings.

```java
public class T1 {
    public static void main(String[] args) {
        System.out.println("Welcome to Java");
        System.out.println("Welcome to Java");
        System.out.println("Welcome to Java");
        System.out.println("Welcome to Java");
        System.out.println("Welcome to Java");
    }
}
```

```java
public class T01 {
    public static void main(String[] args){

        for(int i = 0; i < 5; i++){
            System.out.println("Welcome To Java");
        }


    }
}
```

On the contrary, the classes *TemperatureConverter* and *CurrencyConverter* are similar in form. However, an experienced developer would quickly realize that they calculate different things (temperature vs currencies), so they should not be considered clones. However, their high similarity in form might make many unsupervised measures consider them Category II clones.

```java
public class TemperatureConverter {
    public static double celsiusToFahrenheit(double cels) {
        return cels * 9 / 5 + 32;
    }
}
```

```java
public class CurrencyConverter {
    public static double usdToEur(double usd) {
        return usd * 85 / 100;
    }
}
```

Table 1 compares various unsupervised similarity measures for code analysis. Some of these measures are based on textual similarity, while others are based on the structure of the code. Other measures might analyze the code's functionality beyond just the text or structure. In principle, there is no accurate or inaccurate result in this context. However, intuition tells us that some measures may better serve our purposes. The ideal result would be 1.00 in the first column and 0.00 in the second. Nevertheless, any result that can discern clones (giving them a high similarity value) from non-clones (giving them a low similarity value) would be good.

Table 1. Comparison of various unsupervised similarity measures for code similarity measurement

Measure	Score-Ex1.	Score-Ex2.
Abstract Syntax Trees (ASTs) Similarity	0.50	0.81
Bag-of-Words Similarity	0.72	0.65
Code Embeddings Similarity	0.99	1.00
Comments Similarity	1.00	1.00
Fuzzy Matching Similarity	0.54	0.64
Function Calls similarity	1.00	0.00
Graph-based Similarity	0.38	0.34
Jaccard Similarity	0.27	0.35
Levenshtein Similarity	0.51	0.69
Longest Common Subsequence (LCS) Similarity	0.19	0.29
Metrics Similarity	0.98	1.00
N-grams Similarity	0.26	0.14
Output Analysis Similarity	1.00	0.00
Perceptual Hashing Similarity	0.69	0.88
Program Dependence Graph Similarity	1.00	1.00
R.-Karp-Rabin G.-Str.-Til. (RKR-GST) Similarity	0.96	0.83
Rolling Hash Similarity	1.00	0.55
Semdiff Similarity	0.22	0.40
Semantic Clone Similarity	0.54	0.79
TF-IDF Similarity	0.67	0.48
Winnow Similarity	1.00	0.60

Please note that something special happens with the *Comments Similarity* result. Since none of the displayed code fragments have comments, the measure thinks they are similar. This is just an example of why caution is necessary when considering the results.

4   Evaluation

Several aspects come into play when evaluating and comparing unsupervised similarity measures for clone detection. To effectively evaluate these techniques, it is essential to consider the dataset's nature, the clone categories to face, and the task's requirements.

In this way, some measures excel in comparing textual content, making them suitable for detecting cloned text. Other techniques are more apt for identifying similar functionality. In contrast, other measures can assist in uncovering structural similarities between code and text. The choice depends on the nature of the data in the benchmark dataset.

4.1 Dataset

We are using here the IR-Plag dataset[1] which is designed to serve as a benchmark for evaluating and comparing the performance of different strategies [21]. This dataset includes plagiarized code files deliberately crafted to mimic academic plagiarism behaviors. Although the dataset is compiled to detect plagiarism, it is valid for our purposes since the practical result of plagiarism and cloning is the same in practice, even if their original intentionality might differ (intention to deceive in the first case, no intentionality in the second). Moreover, this dataset does not merely focus on simplistic plagiarism attacks but encompasses a complete range of complexities. Although this dataset does not classify clones, it can be useful in detecting suitable semantic similarity measures for mitigating code redundancy and duplication within complex software projects.

In analyzing a dataset of code files, we observe the following metrics: The dataset contains seven original code files (original programming assignments). A high number of files, 355 (77%), are identified as plagiarized, suggesting a considerable prevalence of duplication. There are 105 non-plagiarized files, which might represent modified or derivative works. The total count of code files in the dataset is 467. Within these files are 59,201 tokens, with 540 distinct tokens, indicating the variety of programming language elements used. The size of the files varies significantly, with the largest file containing 286 tokens and the smallest comprising 40 tokens. On average, a code file in this dataset includes around 126 tokens. These insights show the dataset's composition, reflecting a great diversity in programming syntax.

4.2 Results

In the following, we show the results obtained from the experiments on the IR-Plag dataset. We look primarily at the accuracy (hit percentage) and the execution time required as we believe these are two of the most important aspects to consider when considering putting a measure into operation. These results can be reproduced with the provided source code[2].

On the one hand, Fig. 1 compares the different measures. The horizontal axis quantifies the accuracy of each measure, while the vertical axis lists the unsupervised measures. *Output Analysis* has the highest accuracy score, which could imply that it is most effective at detecting code that performs the same function despite differences in implementation. Contrariwise, *LCS* has the lowest accuracy score, indicating that it might not be as effective in this comparison.

---

[1] https://github.com/oscarkarnalim/sourcecodeplagiarismdataset.
[2] https://github.com/jorge-martinez-gil/codesim.

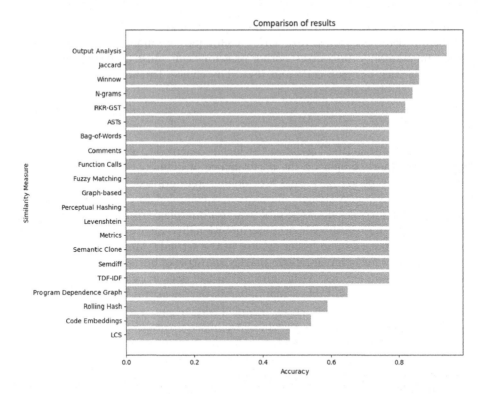

Fig. 1. Accuracy of the unsupervised semantic similarity measures when performing clone detection

It is essential to note that the dataset contains 77% clones. Therefore, a simplistic approach could be to classify all comparisons as clones, which would result in achieving an accuracy of 0.77 by default. This would not be a good result. Figure 1 shows that only using 5 measures produces a real gain over that base result.

On the other hand, Fig. 2 presents a comparative analysis of various measures used to execute code, measured by their execution time. The horizontal axis quantifies the execution time, while the vertical axis lists the unsupervised measures. The *Output Analysis* shows the longest execution time, significantly outpacing other methods such as *Comments* and *Code Embeddings*. The remaining measures show lower execution times, suggesting a more efficient performance. Two facts can be immediately deduced from these experiments:

1. First, only five of the measures studied (i.e., *Output Analysis*, *Winnow*, *N-grams*, *RKR-GST*, and *Jaccard*) help identify clones effectively. This suggests that most unsupervised semantic similarity measures are not helpful in the current form. Therefore, more research on innovative approaches to clone detection is needed.

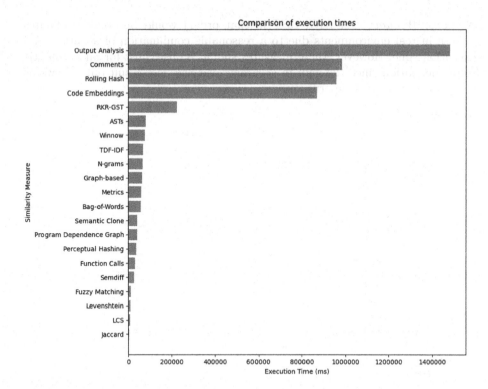

Fig. 2. Execution time of the unsupervised semantic similarity measures when performing clone detection

2. Despite being excellent in accuracy (e.g., *Output Analysis*), some techniques incur such a high computational cost that incorporating them into a practical, real-world tool for programmers becomes unrealistic. The reason *Output Analysis* takes so much execution time is that it must take the two pieces of code, encapsulate them for compilation, pass some random parameters to them (if necessary), and compare the outputs produced. This entire process is very computationally expensive.

   Other time-consuming similarity measures are *Rolling Hash* (very intensive in the use of mathematical operations), *Comments Similarity* (identifying comments involves the use of regular expressions, which is computationally expensive), and *Code Embeddings* (which needs to search and identify embeddings as well as perform operations on them). Therefore, it would be possible to define a feasibility index that calculates a combination of accuracy and execution time to elucidate which measures could work well in real environments. This could be done by weighing the importance of accuracy about time and dividing the result by the total execution time.

   Figure 3 shows us the calculation of the feasibility index. We consider the accuracy importance over the execution time as 10:1. Therefore, just *Jaccard,*

N-grams, *Winnow*, and *RKR-GST*(in that order) would be good candidates for use in real environments due to a reasonable combination of accuracy and execution time. However, these measures should be used just for an automatic recommendation since the gain in accuracy over the base result only allows us to operate them with supervision.

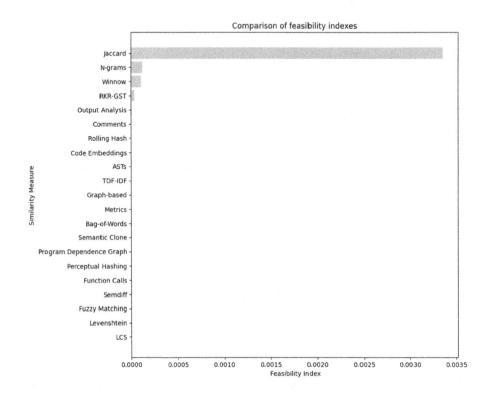

Fig. 3. Comparison of the feasibility index of the unsupervised methods

4.3   Other Metrics

Apart from accuracy, there are other metrics from the information retrieval field to assess how well a clone detection system performs in terms of accuracy and completeness.

– Precision: The approach's accuracy is evaluated by measuring the proportion of correctly identified true clones among all identified code fragments. Higher precision means greater reliability.
– Recall: Recall, also known as sensitivity, assesses the approach's completeness. It quantifies the proportion of true clones in the dataset that were successfully identified. A higher recall indicates fewer missed clones.

- F-measure: The F-measure evaluates overall performance by balancing precision and recall. It ensures a well-rounded assessment of both precision and
  recall.

This way of evaluating is also popular since it gives more weight to the positive classes by considering false positives (precision) and false negatives (recall)
separately. It penalizes the model for failing to detect positive cases and making
false positive predictions.

Table 2 shows us the results that can be obtained for these metrics from the
information retrieval field with the unsupervised similarity measures that we
have been using throughout this work.

Table 2. Comparison of the unsupervised semantic similarity measures using other
popular metrics

Measure	Precision	Recall	F-Measure
Abstract Syntax Trees (ASTs) Similarity	0.77	0.78	0.78
Bag-of-Words Similarity	0.79	0.66	0.72
Code Embeddings Similarity	0.75	0.34	0.47
Comments Similarity	0.77	1.00	0.87
Function Calls similarity	0.78	0.91	0.84
Fuzzy Matching Similarity	0.77	1.00	0.87
Graph-based Similarity	0.80	0.52	0.63
Jaccard Similarity	0.81	0.94	0.87
Levenshtein Similarity	0.80	0.66	0.72
Longest Common Subsequence (LCS) Similarity	0.74	0.06	0.11
Metrics Similarity	0.77	1.00	0.87
N-grams Similarity	0.84	0.29	0.43
Output Analysis Similarity	0.85	0.97	0.90
Perceptual Hashing Similarity	0.77	0.85	0.81
Program Dependence Graph Similarity	0.85	0.39	0.53
R.-Karp-Rabin G.-Str.-Til. (RKR-GST) Similarity	0.79	0.99	0.88
Rolling Hash Similarity	0.93	0.18	0.30
Semdiff Similarity	0.79	0.38	0.51
Semantic Clone Similarity	0.79	0.68	0.73
TF-IDF Similarity	0.77	0.99	0.87
Winnow Similarity	0.81	0.98	0.88

As can be seen, the *Code Embeddings Similarity* approach stands out with
the highest precision, indicating its remarkable accuracy in identifying code
clones. For comprehensive clone detection, *Output Analysis Similarity* and *Program Dependence Graph Similarity* excel with good recall values, implying their

ability to capture a significant portion of true clones. We exclude *Comments Similarity* for reasons already commented about the dataset's low importance of comments.

If we look for a balanced performance that combines precision and recall, *Output Analysis Similarity* offers an attractive option, boasting the highest F-Measure at 0.90. Exactly as was the case with accuracy; however, its high execution times would still give it no option in exploitation environments, so *Jaccard*, *RKR-GST*, and *Winnow* would be, again, more suitable. In this occasion, *N-grams* should not be considered due to its low recall.

5 Discussion

Our experiments show that a reduced group of unsupervised source code similarity measurements could be used to detect source code clones. These methods could improve various aspects of software engineering. For example, they could suggest the existence of clones and, therefore, present an opportunity to refactor the code into reusable parts. This might facilitate code reuse, which is vital in software engineering.

It is also necessary to remark that noisy and unstructured code environments characterize real-world computing environments. We have identified several unsupervised similarity measures that have shown promise in managing this noise and variability, making them valuable when labeled data is limited or impractical. However, the majority of similarity measures studied would not be suitable for this purpose.

Despite some progress, our research still needs to solve several challenges. These include achieving cross-language similarity measurement and ensuring scalability for large codebases. These challenges present compelling opportunities for future research. This means that our research results, although slightly applicable in their current form, need further research to be useful as software development advances into a more automated future.

6 Conclusion

The challenge of source code clone detection represents a very important aspect of software engineering that impacts many diverse applications. In this work, we have evaluated the existing unsupervised similarity measures to address the challenges of the absence of labeled data and diverse coding styles. Our research illustrates how unsupervised source code similarity measurement can facilitate clone detection.

As codebases grow, developing accurate and efficient unsupervised similarity measures remains an essential area of exploration for the community. Furthermore, the need for effective unsupervised techniques will likely expand as the software industry evolves. Although studying supervised techniques may promise good results, unsupervised techniques will always be an option due to their more realistic requirements, adaptability, interpretability, and efficiency.

Therefore, the future of source code clone detection using unsupervised measures holds notable promise. Future efforts could focus on hybrid approaches that integrate the strengths of different methods (a.k.a. ensembles), leading to more robust and accurate similarity assessments. Exploring transfer learning techniques could also improve performance. The goal should be to enhance strategies for code analysis with good accuracy but minimal human intervention.

Acknowledgments. The author thanks all the anonymous reviewers for their help in improving the manuscript. The research reported in this paper has been funded by the Federal Ministry for Climate Action, Environment, Energy, Mobility, Innovation and Technology (BMK), the Federal Ministry for Labour and Economy (BMAW), and the State of Upper Austria in the frame of the SCCH competence center INTEGRATE [(FFG grant no. 892418)] in the COMET - Competence Centers for Excellent Technologies Programme managed by Austrian Research Promotion Agency FFG.

References

1. Ul Ain, Q., Butt, W.H., Anwar, M.W., Azam, F., Maqbool, B.: A systematic review on code clone detection. IEEE Access **7**, 86121–86144 (2019)
2. Alon, U., Zilberstein, M., Levy, O., Yahav, E.: code2vec: learning distributed representations of code. In: Proceedings of the ACM on Programming Languages, vol. 3(POPL), pp. 1–29 (2019)
3. Aniceto, R.C., Holanda, M., Castanho, C., Da Silva, D.: Source code plagiarism detection in an educational context: a literature mapping. In: 2021 IEEE Frontiers in Education Conference (FIE), pp. 1–9. IEEE (2021)
4. Baxter, I.D., et al.: Clone detection using abstract syntax trees. In: 1998 International Conference on Software Maintenance, ICSM 1998, Bethesda, Maryland, USA, November 16–19, 1998, pp. 368–377. IEEE Computer Society (1998)
5. Bellon, S., Koschke, R., Antoniol, G., Krinke, J., Merlo, E.: Comparison and evaluation of clone detection tools. IEEE Trans. Softw. Eng. **33**(9), 577–591 (2007)
6. Bergroth, L., Hakonen, H., Raita, T.: A survey of longest common subsequence algorithms. In: Proceedings Seventh International Symposium on String Processing and Information Retrieval. SPIRE 2000, pp. 39–48. IEEE (2000)
7. Corley, C.D., Mihalcea, R.: Measuring the semantic similarity of texts. In: Proceedings of the ACL Workshop on Empirical Modeling of Semantic Equivalence and Entailment, pp. 13–18 (2005)
8. Damashek, M.: Gauging similarity with n-grams: language-independent categorization of text. Science **267**(5199), 843–848 (1995)
9. Dang, Y., Ge, S., Huang, R., Zhang, D.: Code clone detection experience at microsoft. In: Proceedings of the 5th International Workshop on Software Clones, pp. 63–64 (2011)
10. Devlin, J., Chang, M.-W., Lee, K., Toutanova, K.: BERT: pre-training of deep bidirectional transformers for language understanding. In: Burstein, J., Doran, C., Solorio, T., (eds.), Proceedings of the 2019 Conference of the North American Chapter of the Association for Computational Linguistics: Human Language Technologies, NAACL-HLT 2019, Minneapolis, MN, USA, June 2–7, 2019, Volume 1 (Long and Short Papers), pp. 4171–4186. Association for Computational Linguistics (2019)

11. Dou, S., et al.: Towards understanding the capability of large language models on code clone detection: a survey. arXiv preprint arXiv:2308.01191 (2023)

12. Ferrante, J., Ottenstein, K.J., Warren, J.D.: The program dependence graph and its use in optimization. ACM Trans. Programm. Lang. Syst. (TOPLAS) **9**(3), 319–349 (1987)

13. Gabel, M., Jiang, L., Su, Z.: Scalable detection of semantic clones. In: Proceedings of the 30th International Conference on Software Engineering, pp. 321–330 (2008)

14. Haque, S., Eberhart, Z., Bansal, A., McMillan, C.: Semantic similarity metrics for evaluating source code summarization. In: Proceedings of the 30th IEEE/ACM International Conference on Program Comprehension, pp. 36–47 (2022)

15. Hartanto, A.D., Syaputra, A., Pristyanto, Y.: Best parameter selection of Rabin-Karp algorithm in detecting document similarity. In: 2019 International Conference on Information and Communications Technology (ICOIACT), pp. 457–461. IEEE (2019)

16. Higo, Y., Ueda, Y., Kamiya, T., Kusumoto, S., Inoue, K.: On software maintenance process improvement based on code clone analysis. In: Oivo, M., Komi-Sirviö, S. (eds.) PROFES 2002. LNCS, vol. 2559, pp. 185–197. Springer, Heidelberg (2002). https://doi.org/10.1007/3-540-36209-6_17

17. Horwitz, S.: Identifying the semantic and textual differences between two versions of a program. In: Proceedings of the ACM SIGPLAN 1990 Conference on Programming Language Design and Implementation, pp. 234–245 (1990)

18. Juergens, E., Deissenboeck, F., Hummel, B., Wagner, S.: Do code clones matter? In: 2009 IEEE 31st International Conference on Software Engineering, pp. 485–495. IEEE (2009)

19. Karnalim, O.: TF-IDF inspired detection for cross-language source code plagiarism and collusion. Comput. Sci. **21**, 1–24 (2020)

20. Karnalim, O.: Explanation in code similarity investigation. IEEE Access **9**, 59935–59948 (2021)

21. Karnalim, O., Budi, S., Toba, H., Joy, M.: Source code plagiarism detection in academia with information retrieval: dataset and the observation. Inform. Educ. **18**(2), 321–344 (2019)

22. Karnalim, O., Simon: Syntax trees and information retrieval to improve code similarity detection. In: Proceedings of the Twenty-Second Australasian Computing Education Conference, pp. 48–55 (2020)

23. Krinke, J.: Identifying similar code with program dependence graphs. In: Proceedings Eighth Working Conference on Reverse Engineering, pp. 301–309. IEEE (2001)

24. Levenshtein, V.I.: Binary codes capable of correcting deletions, insertions, and reversals. In: Soviet physics doklady, vol. 10, pp. 707–710 (1966)

25. Martinez-Gil, J.: Semantic similarity aggregators for very short textual expressions: a case study on landmarks and points of interest. J. Intell. Inf. Syst. **53**(2), 361–380 (2019)

26. Martinez-Gil, J.: A comprehensive review of stacking methods for semantic similarity measurement. Mach. Learn. App. **10**, 100423 (2022)

27. Martinez-Gil, J., Chaves-Gonzalez, J.M.: Semantic similarity controllers: on the trade-off between accuracy and interpretability. Knowl. Based Syst. **234**, 107609 (2021)

28. Martinez-Gil, J., Chaves-Gonzalez, J.M.: A novel method based on symbolic regression for interpretable semantic similarity measurement. Expert Syst. Appl. **160**, 113663 (2020)

29. Novak, M., Joy, M., Kermek, D.: Source-code similarity detection and detection tools used in academia: a systematic review. ACM Trans. Comput. Educ. (TOCE) **19**(3), 1–37 (2019)

30. Nuñez-Varela, A.S., Pérez-Gonzalez, H.G., Martínez-Perez, F.E., Soubervielle-Montalvo, C.: Source code metrics: a systematic mapping study. J. Syst. Softw. **128**, 164–197 (2017)

31. Peters, M.E., et al.: Deep contextualized word representations. In: Walker, M.A. Ji, H., Stent, A., (eds.), Proceedings of the 2018 Conference of the North American Chapter of the Association for Computational Linguistics: Human Language Technologies, NAACL-HLT 2018, New Orleans, Louisiana, USA, June 1–6, 2018, Volume 1 (Long Papers), pp. 2227–2237. Association for Computational Linguistics (2018)

32. Ragkhitwetsagul, C., Krinke, J., Marnette, B.: A picture is worth a thousand words: code clone detection based on image similarity. In: 12th IEEE International Workshop on Software Clones, IWSC 2018, Campobasso, Italy, March 20, 2018, pp. 44–50. IEEE Computer Society (2018)

33. Roy, C.K., Cordy, J.R., Koschke, R.: Comparison and evaluation of code clone detection techniques and tools: a qualitative approach. Sci. Comput. Programm. **74**(7), 470–495 (2009)

34. Roy, C.K., Cordy, J.R.: A survey on software clone detection research. Queen's School Comput. TR. **541**(115), 64–68 (2007)

35. Saini, N., Singh, S., et al.: Code clones: detection and management. Proc. Comput. Sci. **132**, 718–727 (2018)

36. Schleimer, S., Wilkerson, D.S., Aiken, A.: Winnowing: local algorithms for document fingerprinting. In: Proceedings of the 2003 ACM SIGMOD International Conference on Management of Data, pp. 76–85 (2003)

37. Singla, N., Garg, D.: String matching algorithms and their applicability in various applications. Int. J. Soft Comput. Eng. **1**(6), 218–222 (2012)

38. Wise, M.J.: String similarity via greedy string tiling and running Karp-Rabin matching. Online Preprint **119**(1), 1–17 (1993)

39. Ming, X.: A similarity metric method of obfuscated malware using function-call graph. J. Comput. Virol. Hacking Techn. **9**, 35–47 (2013)

40. Zager, L.A., Verghese, G.C.: Graph similarity scoring and matching. Appl. Math. Lett. **21**(1), 86–94 (2008)

Continuous Integration and Deployment

Using Datalog for Effective Continuous Integration Policy Evaluation

Kaarel Loide[2], Bruno Rucy Carneiro Alves de Lima[1,2]($\boxtimes$) [iD], Pelle Jakovits[1], and Jevgeni Demidov[2]

[1] University of Tartu, Narva mnt 18, Tartu, Estonia
{bruno98,jakovits}@ut.ee
[2] Pipedrive, New York, USA
{kaarel.loide,rucy.carneiro,jevgeni.demidov}@pipedrive.com

Abstract. Containerisation and microservices have introduced unprecedented complexity in system configurations, exacerbating the blast zone of misconfigurations and system failures. This complexity is further amplified within the DevOps paradigm, where developers are entrusted with the entire software development lifecycle, often without comprehensive insights into the impact of their configurations. This article explores using the declarative logic programming language Datalog in automating and optimizing configuration validation to mitigate these challenges.

We present an overview of a real-world case involving a software company with approximately 300 engineers, highlighting the challenges that lead to delegating mission-critical configuration validation to a declarative language.

With Datalog, we spearheaded an initiative to entirely deprecate a non-declarative solution in order to attempt to circumvent the problem of writing business logic alongside its evaluation. The outcome revealed a substantial reduction in maintenance efforts and user complaints, providing further evidence of Datalog's potential in streamlining internal policy enforcement.

We propose a set of best practices, extrapolated from our findings, to guide organizations in both implementing and optimizing automatic configuration validation. These insights offer a strategic roadmap for harnessing declarative languages like Datalog to effectively navigate the intricate configuration landscapes of contemporary software systems.

Keywords: Configuration Validation · Symbolic Reasoning · Datalog

1 Introduction

Misconfigurations significantly contribute to failures in contemporary software systems [10,20]. The migration towards cloud-based systems and microservice architectures has exacerbated this issue, amplifying the complexity and volume of configurations required for optimal system performance.

P. Bludau et al. (Eds.): SWQD 2024, LNBIP 505, pp. 41–52, 2024.
https://doi.org/10.1007/978-3-031-56281-5_3

The integration of third-party components like Apache Kafka [1] and Redis [6], each demanding intricate tuning of numerous parameters, further complicates the configuration landscape [21]. In larger corporations, the multiplicity of services, each deployed across diverse regions with distinct configuration needs, escalates this complexity.

Traditionally, DevOps [14] teams shouldered the responsibility of managing these configurations. However, ever-increasing complexity inevitably leads to the responsibility of some of these tasks to fall on developers. This shift, though pragmatic, introduces challenges. Developers, while adept at managing their services, often lack the expertise to configure the supporting infrastructure effectively.

The integration of automatic deployment processes, while enhancing efficiency, amplifies the risk of propagating configuration errors. A minor oversight can swiftly escalate, compromising the entire application's integrity and performance. Misconfigurations not only pose a threat to application stability but perhaps more importantly disrupt developers' workflows, imposing a cognitive load that undermines productivity [9].

Security remains another critical concern. Complex cloud-native platforms like Kubernetes [5] and Docker [2] present ample opportunities for oversights that expose systems and networks to security breaches.

The introduction of automatic configuration validation within the continuous integration/continuous deployment (CI/CD) process emerges as a viable solution. The diversity in organizational setups however, and the need for customized policy enforcement complicates this, as there are four seemingly independent research questions to answer:

1. **How to describe configuration policies in code?**
2. **How to evaluate policies with respect to arbitrary data?**
3. **How to ensure that policy evaluation is correct?**
4. **How to test the policy evaluation code?**

The novelty of our contribution lies in modelling the first question as a symbolic reasoning problem using the logic programming language Datalog [12], and then in investigating how answers to the other questions could naturally arise. We provide evidence to the practical usefulness of this paradigm shift both from the viewpoint of those writing the code that validates configuration, and from the end-users whose code gets validated.

2   Related Works

An promising direction for Configuration validation has been in shifting from manual and ad hoc approaches to more structured and declarative methods. The seminal work in this field is Microsoft's ConfValley [13], which emphasized the benefits of using a rule-based language for configuration validation. Their approach significantly reduced the amount of code required, as seen in cases where thousands of lines of imperative code were replaced with over a hundred lines of declarative code.

However, due to the nature of its expressive core formalism, CPL, ConfValley identified challenges in handling dynamic configuration elements, an aspect that is important in our setting. By employing a top-down compiler [4] for a less expressive language, extended with a restricted form of dynamic rules, we manage both static and dynamic aspects in a way that our needs are addressed.

Contrasting this approach with machine learning-based methods such as outlier detection [16,18] and more robust configuration testing [23], using Datalog offered a seamless and scalable solution to our situation, as the way our system worked would not change, only its implementation would.

The rise of Large Language Models (LLMs) [22] in configuration validation introduces new possibilities, yet they come with their own set of challenges, primarily such as ensuring output reliability [15,19], which are unacceptable as being part of a system for strict policy enforcement.

By leveraging Datalog in a industrial setting of significant scale, we contribute to the ongoing evolution towards declarative quality assurance, showcasing its successful in superseding of an imperative system, furthering the arguments laid down in [13].

3   Background

Datalog is a declarative language with semantics denoting the evaluation of a set of possibly-recursive restricted horn clauses, a program, over a set of facts. Evaluating a program Π entails computing all implicit consequences over a fact store E, yielding new facts. A Program is a set of rules of the following form:

$$\mathbf{h}(x_1, ..., x_j) \leftarrow \bigwedge_{i=1}^{k} \mathbf{b}_i(x_1, ..., x_j) \qquad (1)$$

We label h as the head atom, containing x_i terms that can be either constant or variable, and $B = \bigwedge_{i=1} b_i$ as the body with each b_i being an atom.

Example 1. Graph reachability as a Datalog program

$\Pi = \{\mathbf{reaches}(?x, ?y) \leftarrow \mathbf{connected}(?x, ?y),$
$\qquad \mathbf{reaches}(?x, ?z) \leftarrow \mathbf{reaches}(?x, ?y), \mathbf{reaches}(?y, ?z)\}$
$E = \{\mathbf{connected} = \{("a", "b"), ("b", "c"), ("c", "d")\}\}$
$\Pi(E) = \{\mathbf{reaches} = \{("a", "b"), ("b", "c"), ("c", "d"), ("a", "c"), ("a", "d"), ("b", "d")\}\}$

Example 1 demonstrates Datalog's minimal syntax alongside the result $\Pi(E)$ of evaluating program Π over a set of facts E. Π has two rules. The first one reads as *For all x, y that are connected, it follows that y is reachable from x*. The second extends the meaning of **reaches** to be transitive: *For all x, y, z, if x reaches y, and y reaches z, then it follows that z is reachable from x*. Evaluating the first rule will yield one new **reaches** fact for every fact in **connected**. The second rule implies recursion, as **reaches** depends in itself. Its evaluation will recur until no more facts can be generated. $("a", "c")$ and $("a", "d")$ are **reaches** facts that stem directly from the second rule. Datalog's declarativeness and exact recursive semantics offer a natural medium for concisely denoting complex general policies over arbitrary domains. So long as one writes policies in Datalog, their evaluation is guaranteed to be correct.

As Datalog is primarily a mathematical formalism, with no standard implementation, the choice of implementation is highly reliant on which additional features are needed. Our requirements all stem from the sake of system integration. Pipedrive has over 1400 git repositories that have some level of homogeneity, with every single one of them needing to adhere to CI policies. Additional enterprise related requirements were that the solution must support safe secret injection, http requests, and rule testability. An interesting remark is that none of these features, and their impact in Datalog semantics, have been investigated in recent literature.

3.1   Open Policy Agent

Open Policy Agent [4] (OPA) is a high-performance top-down Datalog engine with JSON [11] semantics, that to this date, remains the most popular implementation on Github [8]. In standard a Datalog program 1, each atom b_i is comprised of a predicate p_i representing a relation, alongside terms $x_1, ..., x_n$ that can either be constant or variable. b_i represents an assumption that $(x_1, ..., x_j) \in p_i$ holds, and if each b_i holds, then h, the head atom, holds. Relations are modelled as subsets of a single JSON document J e.g given { person: { hobbies: ["dancing"] } }, then $hobbies \subset J$. Atoms are existential constraints over both the JSON structure and declared variables.

The main diversion is in disallowing recursion, therefore significantly lowering the bar for it to be performant. We point out that it does support however, negation and arbitrary user functions, that are more important to porting our existing rules than recursion.

3.2   Rego

Rego is the official name for OPA's Datalog syntax. It detracts in numerous ways from usual Datalog by providing extensive syntactic sugars, most of them pertaining to traversing JSON.

```
devServers {
    some site in sites
    site.name == "dev"
    every server in site.servers {
        endswith(server.name, "-dev")
    }
}
```

Listing 1.1. Simple rego rule

Listing 1.1 showcases rule **devServers**. A possible interpretation of it in Datalog extended with both equality and **endsWith** predicates could be:

$$\textbf{hasDevServer}("dev", ?x) \leftarrow \textbf{sites}(?x), \textbf{servers}(?x, ?y),$$
$$\textbf{equals}(?x, "dev"), \textbf{endsWith}(?y, "\text{-}dev")$$

It provides a specialized and succinct syntax for non-recursive reasoning over JSON documents.

4   Use Case

The company is an international cloud-based software as a service (SaaS) provider that offers a customer relationship management (CRM) tool for small to medium-sized business. The company employs over 300 software engineers, that develop a distributed application deployed on Kubernetes consisted of approximately 750 microservices. Given that it has existed for ten years, there have been multiple technologies and best practices developed. It is paramount that each microservice adheres to these.

All policies stem from the most atomic requirement; microservices must be correctly and securely configured as containerised applications. Building these container images ought to be done through Dockerfiles [7], and their deployment on Kubernetes must be outlined with a templating solution. Furthermore, all code repositories live in Github, and each team within the company must follow all guidelines relating to repository hygiene.

Our continuous integration system is also directly located on Github. Whenever work on any microservice occurs, the designated engineer creates a separate branch from the repository main branch. After the work is finished, a pull request to merge it to the master branch (that represents the live state of the application) is created. It is in this crucial moment that automated policy enforcement must occur, for as after the code gets merged, it will be immediately deployed to live environments.

4.1   Dora

The tool that was in place before the introduction of Datalog was called Deployment or Repository Analyzer (Dora) [17]. At first, its core responsibility was to analyse docker and docker-compose (a system to run multiple docker containers locally) files and validate them. Over time, Dora drifted from its original purpose and became a general policy enforcement engine.

```
module.exports = async function (config) {
  try {
    // Negative Lookahead on comments line
    const key = '^(?!#)${config.param}';
    // Get Base image from Dockerfile.CI
    const dockerfileCIResults = await findStringByKey(config, key);
    const dockerFileConfig = { path: 'Dockerfile', param: config.param };
    const dockerfileResults = await findStringByKey(dockerFileConfig, key);
```

```
if (dockerfileCIResults.length > 0) {
  // Compare the last FROM occurency for both files
  const baseImageCI = dockerfileCIResults.slice(-1)[0].line.value;
  if (dockerfileResults.length > 0) {
    // Image found in both files
    const baseDevImage = dockerfileResults.slice(-1)[0].line.value.trim()
;
    if (baseImageCI !== baseDevImage && `${baseImageCI}-dev` !==
baseDevImage && !isGoService()) {
        await reporter.report(config, dockerfileCIResults.slice(-1)[0].line
);
    }
  } else {
    // Image found only in Dockerfile.CI
    await reporter.report(config, dockerfileCIResults.slice(-1)[0].line);
  }
} else {
  if (dockerfileResults.length > 0) {
    // Image found only in Dockerfile
    await reporter.report(config, dockerfileResults.slice(-1)[0].line);
  }
}
} catch (err) {
  const error = `Error message: ${err}`;
  await reporter.reportError(error, config);
}
};
```

Listing 1.2. Imperative configuration validation in Javascript

Dora was written in Javascript as a command line interface. Listing 1.2 exhibits an actual example of a Dora rule, and serves as a strong motivation to use declarative languages, due to its brittleness and mixture of concerns i.e. business logic is mixed with rule evaluation logic. The rule definition has four steps, the first seeks two Dockerfiles in some microservice repository to then load them in memory and compare their parent image. The final part is to report the error.

Only the third part, where the comparison between the two images occurs, relates to the logic of the rule itself. That is, 97% of all code is boilerplate. The impact of not separating rule logic from else was always felt when attempting to debug erratic behavior. It is not straightforward to deduct whether an issue stemmed from faulty logic, or from all other code.

4.2   Neodora

```
imageDefinition[result] {
  data.neodora.files["go.mod"] == null
  ciImage := parent_image(input)
  normalImage := trim_suffix(parent_image(data.neodora.files.Dockerfile), "-
    dev")
  ciImage != normalImage
  result = {
    "ciImage": ciImage,
    "normalImage": normalImage,
  }
}
```

Listing 1.3. Listing 1.2's logic translated to Rego

The core of Neodora, Dora's reimagination, is OPA. Listing 1.3 showcases the same rule as in Listing 1.2, but written with Rego. None of the aforementioned issues exist. Engineers are only responsible for outlining logic. This greatly reduces the room for error and eases debugging.

The rule will only be true if there is a mismatch between images. Repositories are checked for all rules by injecting the needed files as ground facts. Auxiliary files, decided on a per-rule specification, live under `files`, while `input` represents the primary source of ground facts. A repository is considered to pass all CI standards if no rule is true.

```
test_deny_different_images {
  imageDefinition[{
    "ciImage": "node:14-alpine",
    "normalImage": "php:16-alpine",
  }] with input as [[{
      "Cmd": "from",
      "Value": ["node:14-alpine"],
    }]]
    with data.neodora.files as {
      "go.mod": null,
      "Dockerfile": [[{ "Cmd": "from", "Value": ["php:16-alpine"] }]],
    }
}
```

Listing 1.4. Testing Datalog with Datalog

OPA's key Datalog extension, for usage in enterprise scenarios, is its extensive support for testing rules. While there is significant research in provenance of Datalog programs [24], testing mechanisms have not been thoroughly investigated. Listing 1.4 shows a rule that tests the rule from Listing 1.3, by querying it while overwriting its dependencies.

The previous implementation had a suite of functional tests to verify rules. This suite required the developer to use a single mock repository to describe a failing set of configurations and a single mock repository to define a set of passing configurations. Dora was then executed against these mock repositories to verify rule by checking that the failing repository had a failure for each rule and the passing repository had no failures reported.

While this provided some validation, it quickly became hard to follow as mock data for different configurations is clumped into the same repository. It also made testing different failure cases for a single rule impossible as there is only a single input for each execution. As long as the test suite finds one failure case, the tests will pass. Furthermore, this test suite provided no coverage information, hence it being difficult to enforce any quality standards on rules.

OPA provides a much improved solution to this, with both unit testing and coverage features as previously mentioned, alongside the testing of each rule being independent of other rules being tested. This significantly increased the reliability of our CI system. Figure 1 portrays the architecture of Neodora, and highlights the complex surrounding tooling that is necessary to integrate a domain-specific language to a modern enterprise architecture. A major advantage of Dora, was that given that it was built in Javascript, a language which is thoroughly used not only internally, with extensive libraries and integrations, but in general, much pre-existing tooling was available, hence the time-to-live of that solution was almost immediate.

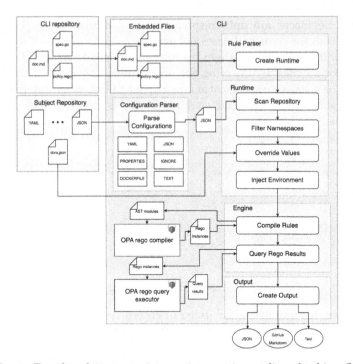

Fig. 1. Datalog-driven continuous integration policy checking flow

Meanwhile, Neodora was written in Go, primarily to ease the integration with OPA, that too is a Go project. In spite of there having being no internal standardized solution to bootstrap go projects, the fully-functioning solution was delivered in less than two months. No developers aside from one out of four had any prior experience with Datalog.

The complexity of the application lies in that its entrypoint is threefold, and requires two compilation phases. One for Neodora's CLI, and another for OPA to compile rules, which happens during Neodora's runtime. The first entrypoint is when the CLI itself is compiled. Rego rules are embedded as strings alongside their specification.

Rule compilation then happens during execution, with their specification denoting values that ought to be injected into OPA both during rule compilation, and later in runtime. Due to the not-absolute homogeinity across all 1400 repositories, it is paramount that each repository should be able to dictate whether certain rules apply to them or not, hence an override file is read during runtime. Lastly, Neodora is invoked per repository, hence the inputs to each rule must be collected after their compilation, but before their execution.

5   Results

In this section, the results of a comparative analysis of Dora with Neodora are presented. The first area of evaluation is rule expressivity, where we report whether

Neodora managed to port all already-existing rules, and how did it cope with new ones. The date stems from first-hand reports of engineers that attempted to do so.

The second area is maintainability. We have collected metrics from the static code analysis software Sonarqube [3] and compared metrics that measure code smells and technical debt resolution estimation. We used the latest code for both repositories. And also took testing coverage into account.

The last area is reliability, where we collect feedback gathered from Slack messages of developers requesting for help or advice when faced with a rule violation. We compare Neodora's most recent data with the most recent data available from Dora that matches the same time range.

Expressivity. Neodora has demonstrated its effectiveness across all configuration validation scenarios encountered by us. Thanks to OPA, policy enforcement has significantly been facilitated and improved, and the use of its testing facilities has facilitated the testing and validation of each rule.

Over a span of approximately one and a half years, we have incorporated 18 new rules into Neodora. As previously mentioned, the tool is utilized in CI to prevent code that could lead to either failed builds or deployments. Rapid feedback occurs through the form of pull request comments on GitHub. It is estimated that Neodora has validated code approximately 350,000 times since its introduction.

In contrast to Dora, the team can now conduct comprehensive testing of each new rule before deploying it organization-wide. Each rule can be executed individually against a single repository and unit-tested. Additionally, any new rule or modification to an existing rule can be validated against every repository in the organization to assess its potential impact. We did not have any scenario where a rule could not be implemented. Some of our rules have dynamic components, such as relying on the response of requests, which was not a problem in practice, even though it might be so theoretically.

Maintainability. Various metrics provided by the static analysis platform Sonarqube [3] can be utilized to compare the two solutions. As Rego rules can not be analyzed by Sonarqube, the code coverage comparison is based on a combination of metrics from Sonarqube and the OPA CLI, which is able to analyze test coverage.

Sonarqube reported a total of 152 code smells for Dora, compared to just four for Neodora. Another metric to compare is the time required to resolve technical debt in the project. The time necessary to address Dora's technical debt is 5,724 min longer than Neodora, which equates to approximately four full days or about 12 working days. Sonarqube provides a ratio between the cost to develop the software and the cost to fix it. This ratio has decreased from 3.7 to 0.1.

Combining Sonarqube and OPA CLI measurements provides insight into the coverage of both the Rego code and the CLI tool's code. DORA had 2,262 lines of code with a coverage of 52.9%. In contrast, Neodora had a total of 2,351 lines to cover, with an overall test coverage of 95.3%.

Reliability. While a declarative language like Datalog might initially be more challenging to learn than a more common imperative language like JavaScript, it is ultimately a more suitable and intuitive tool for configuration validation once the implementer becomes familiar with the general concept. This claim is further supported by the fact that since the introduction of the new Rego-based solution, there have only been six messages sent to the DevOps team that express complaints about the tool. Only two of those messages were bug reports. For Dora, looking at the same time frame, up to right before Neodora was released, there were about 53 complaints and 14 bug reports.

6   Threats to Validity

External Threats. The main limitation to the applicability of our paper is its highly context-specific nature. Our research was conducted in a CRM SaaS provider, with over 750 microservices, more than one thousand GitHub repositories, and over 300 engineers. Our findings do likely apply less to small or medium-sized companies that do not have a development environment that is as dynamic.

Internal Threats. Due to our decision of implementing and integrating the system from scratch, potential errors in Datalog rule implementations or in the core system itself could affect our system's effectiveness and reliability. However, given that Neodora has been evaluated over more than a year likely mitigates these concerns to some extent.

Construct Threats. Threats to construct validity in our study arise from the metrics and methods we used to evaluate the effectiveness of the Datalog-based system. Our assessment relied heavily on metrics like code maintainability, number of complaints, and bug reports, which, while indicative, may not fully capture the system's effectiveness in diverse software development scenarios.

7   Conclusion

We have successfully leveraged Datalog for configuration validation. As a Datalog-based DSL, Rego has proven its effectiveness in articulating configuration validation rules within CI processes, demonstrating that non-recursive Datalog sufficed for all of our use cases.

This article presented a thorough overview of the implemented system, Neodora, alongside an analysis of over one and a half years of data. The findings suggest that Datalog has demonstrated superior maintainability and reliability compared to the preceding solution, Dora, that utilized JavaScript for expressing, evaluating, and testing validation rules. We have identified several key practices that have significantly contributed to the success of Neodora, these include:

Not Mixing Validation Code with Implementation Details. Mixing validation logic with other logic, such as parsing, reporting, or evaluation, leads to boundaries becoming increasingly blurry, often causing situations that are very difficult to debug. This was the main pain point that lead us to consider a declarative approach.

Each Rule must be Individually Testable. Making rules testable greatly improves the maintainability of the tooling as well as helps future rule readers understand the purpose of the rules, which is perhaps of greater benefit than tests themselves. The reliability of Neodora is greatly tied to the extensive options to validate the configuration validation code. Declarative languages are not exempt of testing.

Validation Code should have an Emphasis on Readability. In our setting, configuration validation requirements change more often than regular application code, as best practices evolve and requirements enforced by a company change, which implies that such code is read more often. As Neodora's Datalog testing suite is written in Datalog itself, this propelled engineers' understanding of the tool.

Technical Failures should be Separated from Rule Failures, it was paramount for us to provide visibility to the user as to whether their changes were rejected due to failing to comply with policies, or through some other external problem. When using a declarative language, the execution of a valid program will only fail due to logic errors, and not issues with execution, parsing or other tangential problems.

References

1. Apache kafka (2022). https://kafka.apache.org/
2. Isolate containers with a user namespace (2022). https://docs.docker.com/engine/security/userns-remap/
3. Metric definitions (2022). https://docs.sonarqube.org/latest/user-guide/metric-definitions/
4. Open policy agent: Introduction (2022). https://www.openpolicyagent.org/docs/latest/
5. Production-grade container orchestration (2022). https://kubernetes.io/
6. Redis (2022). https://redis.io/
7. Dockerfile reference (2023). https://docs.docker.com/engine/reference/builder/
8. Open policy agent (2023). https://github.com/open-policy-agent/opa
9. Abad, Z.S., Karras, O., Schneider, K., Barker, K., Bauer, M.: Task interruption in software development projects. In: Proceedings of the 22nd International Conference on Evaluation and Assessment in Software Engineering 2018 (2018). https://doi.org/10.1145/3210459.3210471
10. Baset, S., Suneja, S., Bila, N., Tuncer, O., Isci, C.: Usable declarative configuration specification and validation for applications, systems, and cloud. Proceedings of the 18th ACM/IFIP/USENIX Middleware Conference on Industrial Track - Middleware '17 (2017). https://doi.org/10.1145/3154448.3154453
11. Bourhis, P., Reutter, J.L., Suárez, F., Vrgoc, D.: JSON: data model, query languages and schema specification. In: Proceedings of the 36th ACM SIGMOD-SIGACT-SIGAI Symposium on Principles of Database Systems (2017). https://api.semanticscholar.org/CorpusID:18059418

12. Ceri, S., Gottlob, G., Tanca, L.: What you always wanted to know about Datalog (and never dared to ask). IEEE Trans. Knowl. Data Eng. **1**(1), 146–166 (1989). https://doi.org/10.1109/69.43410

13. Huang, P., Bolosky, W.J., Singh, A., Zhou, Y.: Confvalley. In: Proceedings of the Tenth European Conference on Computer Systems (2015). https://doi.org/10.1145/2741948.2741963

14. Leite, L., Rocha, C., Kon, F., Milojicic, D., Meirelles, P.: A survey of DevOps concepts and challenges. ACM Comput. Surv. **52**(6), 1-35 (2019). https://doi.org/10.1145/3359981. cited By 47

15. Lian, X., Chen, Y., Cheng, R., Huang, J., Thakkar, P., Xu, T.: Configuration validation with large language models. arXiv:abs/2310.09690 (2023). https://api.semanticscholar.org/CorpusID:264146437

16. Palatin, N., Leizarowitz, A., Schuster, A., Wolff, R.: Mining for misconfigured machines in grid systems. In: Knowledge Discovery and Data Mining (2006). https://api.semanticscholar.org/CorpusID:52835750

17. Paljasma, T.: Validating docker image and container security using best practices and company policies (2019). https://digikogu.taltech.ee/et/Item/b9367be6-0646-4c2f-b32b-56ee8a024f0d

18. Pranata, A.A., Barais, O., Bourcier, J., Noirie, L.: Misconfiguration discovery with principal component analysis for cloud-native services. In: 2020 IEEE/ACM 13th International Conference on Utility and Cloud Computing (UCC), pp. 269–278 (2020). https://api.semanticscholar.org/CorpusID:230511700

19. Roziere, B., et al.: Code Llama: open foundation models for code. arXiv preprint: arXiv:2308.12950 (2023)

20. Sun, X., Cheng, R., Chen, J., Ang, E., Legunsen, O., Xu, T.: Testing configuration changes in context to prevent production failures. In: OSDI (2020)

21. Tuncer, O., Bila, N., Duri, S., Isci, C., Coskun, A.K.: ConfEX: towards automating software configuration analytics in the cloud. In: 2018 48th Annual IEEE/IFIP International Conference on Dependable Systems and Networks Workshops (DSN-W), pp. 30–33 (2018). https://doi.org/10.1109/DSN-W.2018.00019

22. Wei, J., et al.: Emergent abilities of large language models. arXiv preprint: arXiv:2206.07682 (2022)

23. Xu, T., Legunsen, O.: Configuration testing: testing configuration values as code and with code. arxiv Software Engineering (2019)

24. Zhao, D., Subotic, P., Scholz, B.: Debugging large-scale datalog. ACM Trans. Program. Lang. Syst. (TOPLAS) **42**, 1–35 (2020). https://api.semanticscholar.org/CorpusID:218905148

Communication and Collaboration

On the Interaction Between Software Engineers and Data Scientists When Building Machine Learning-Enabled Systems

Gabriel Busquim, Hugo Villamizar, Maria Julia Lima,
and Marcos Kalinowski[(✉)]

Pontifical Catholic University of Rio de Janeiro, Rio de Janeiro, Brazil
{gbusquim,hvillamizar,kalinowski}@inf.puc-rio.br,
mjulia@tecgraf.puc-rio.br

Abstract. In recent years, Machine Learning (ML) components have been increasingly integrated into the core systems of organizations. Engineering such systems presents various challenges from both a theoretical and practical perspective. One of the key challenges is the effective interaction between actors with different backgrounds who need to work closely together, such as software engineers and data scientists. This paper presents an exploratory case study that aims to understand the current interaction and collaboration dynamics between these two roles in ML projects. We conducted semi-structured interviews with four practitioners with experience in software engineering and data science of a large ML-enabled system project and analyzed the data using reflexive thematic analysis. Our findings reveal several challenges that can hinder collaboration between software engineers and data scientists, including differences in technical expertise, unclear definitions of each role's duties, and the lack of documents that support the specification of the ML-enabled system. We also indicate potential solutions to address these challenges, such as fostering a collaborative culture, encouraging team communication, and producing concise system documentation. This study contributes to understanding the complex dynamics between software engineers and data scientists in ML projects and provides insights for improving collaboration and communication in this context. We encourage future studies investigating this interaction in other projects.

Keywords: Machine Learning · ML-enabled System · Data Science · Software Engineering · Collaboration

P. Bludau et al. (Eds.): SWQD 2024, LNBIP 505, pp. 55–75, 2024.
https://doi.org/10.1007/978-3-031-56281-5_4

1 Introduction

Integrating Machine Learning (ML) components into existing systems has increased as companies seek to leverage vast amounts of data to enhance the business outcomes of their software products. In this paper, we refer to these systems as ML-enabled systems. Typically, the ML component is only a small part of a larger system [1], which usually comprises other components for data collection, model consumption, and infrastructure requirements.

This transition from developing traditional software systems to those integrated with ML components introduces new challenges from the viewpoint of Software Engineering (SE). The development of ML-enabled systems often involves completely separate workflows, as well as different actors [2]: data scientists build ML models while engineers must deploy and integrate them with other services. An ineffective interaction between team members can cause ML mismatches capable of harming the system [3]. This scenario raises the question of whether proper alignment and communication between the actors occurs and how they share responsibilities when developing ML-enabled systems.

Following the guidelines by Runeson *et al.* [4] for case study research in software engineering, we tackle this issue by conducting an exploratory case study focused on two key roles within ML projects: software engineers and data scientists. The selected case concerns an ML-enabled system for Online Dispute Resolution (ODR) created to help parties settle legal disputes in the state of Rio de Janeiro. Beyond describing the team and system context, we conducted semi-structured interviews with four experienced team members, two software engineers and two data scientists, to understand their current interactions, collaboration dynamics, and problems in ML projects. To this end, we asked practitioners about activities covering the development process end-to-end. Our questions range from defining requirements to analyzing data and integrating the ML model with the rest of the system. We transcribed and analyzed the interviews using reflexive thematic analysis [5,6], one of the Thematic Analysis (TA) family methods. This research approach guided us while analyzing the data and finding patterns among the interviewees' points of view.

We divided our findings into five main categories: **requirements**, **planning**, **data management**, **model management**, and **team interaction**. We illustrate the participants' perceptions and the main improvement opportunities they noted for each category. Respondents expressed several challenges regarding their tasks and current collaboration practices. For example, data scientists and software engineers were not always aware of each other's activities, which led to inaccurate planning and errors when integrating the model with the rest of the system. Even though they viewed their relationship positively, they recognized that a more efficient collaboration could have prevented the late discovery of errors in the system. Our main contribution with this work is highlighting the importance of having well-defined responsibilities and collaboration procedures inside teams developing ML-enabled systems. By reporting challenges faced by professionals, we seek to instigate practitioners to evaluate their collaboration practices since the beginning of the project.

2 Background and Related Work

2.1 Challenges in Building ML-Enabled Systems

Villamizar *et al.* [7] define ML-enabled systems as software systems with an ML component. The development of ML-enabled systems presents several challenges that can significantly impact the interaction between team members. This is the case especially for software engineers and data scientists, who often share responsibilities for handling data and deploying models [8]. For example, designing an appropriate architecture for these systems is not trivial, as the team must evaluate factors such as model performance degradation, uncertainty management, and proper integration between the model and other system components [9].

Furthermore, requirements engineering practices for non-ML software development are not entirely applicable when developing systems with an ML component [10]. There is a typical lack of requirements specifications for such systems [11] that provide a clear definition of the input data, expected model outputs, and how the ML component should integrate into the larger system [7]. Without these specifications, data scientists may create models with assumptions that software engineers are unaware of, leading to integration issues when transitioning from development to production.

The different backgrounds of data scientists and software engineers can also impact their interactions. While data scientists may have strong mathematical and statistical skills [12], software engineers have expertise in programming, software design, and system architecture. This diversity can lead to variations in problem-solving approaches. In addition, their cultural differences can also play an important role. While the tasks performed by data scientists revolve around experimentation and dealing with the uncertainty of unpredictable results [2], software engineers often adhere to structured development methodologies. These cultural disparities can cause barriers in a collaborative environment.

2.2 Communication and Collaboration in ML-Enabled Systems

Amershi *et al.* [13] presented a case study with Microsoft software teams to gather best practices for ML engineering. Results showed how respondents consistently cited collaboration as a challenge. Communication and collaboration are also mentioned in papers examining the role of data scientists. Kim *et al.* [12] presented a survey with data science employees at Microsoft to uncover the challenges they face. Some were related to team communication, such as effectively transmitting insights to leaders and achieving agreement among all stakeholders.

Specifically focusing on collaboration, Zhang *et al.* [14] conducted a survey on how data science workers, including data scientists and software engineers, collaborate. The results depicted how data scientists were engaged throughout all steps of data science projects, while software engineers were more involved in core technical activities, such as acquiring data for the model. Lewis *et al.* [3] studied the consequences of ML mismatches between data scientists, software engineers, and operations staff developing ML-enabled systems. They interviewed practitioners to understand examples and recommendations for avoiding these problems. Results showed that most mismatches were related to incorrect assumptions about the model. They also refer to a lack of model specifications and test cases for integration testing. These issues are directly related to the interaction between data scientists and software engineers.

More recently, Mailach and Siegmund [15] investigated sociotechnical challenges for bringing ML-enabled software into production. They identified challenges related to organizational silos, especially between the data science and software engineering teams. The paper reported tension and communication issues when the teams collaborated, which led to production delays. Nahar *et al.* [16] focused on identifying challenges and recommendations for the interaction between software engineers and data scientists. They mapped several collaboration points between the two actors, from project planning to product-model integration. As in Mailach and Siegmund's study [15], participants also reported problems with data scientists working in isolation and communication issues between them and software engineers.

When discussing the state of the art, Nahar *et al.* [16] mentioned they were unaware of other studies examining challenges between software engineers and data scientists. With our work, we intend to expand the literature on this topic and provide additional insights through a case study strategy. Hence, differently from Nahar *et al.*, who covered perspectives from multiple teams from different organizations, we qualitatively analyzed a selected case, providing its context and conducting thematic analysis. Beyond examining the collaboration between data scientists and software engineers, the case study strategy also allowed us to qualitatively understand the responsibilities these actors had during the execution of the selected case project.

3   Case Study Design

We conducted a case study to enhance our comprehension of the interaction and collaboration dynamics between software engineers and data scientists. Hereafter, we describe its design following the guidelines by Runeson *et al.* [4].

3.1   Goal and Research Questions

The goal of this study, described following the Goal-Question-Metric (GQM) template for goal definition [17], can be seen in Table 1. From this goal, we derived the following research questions.

RQ1: How do software engineers and data scientists share responsibilities when developing an ML-enabled system?

This research question focuses on how responsibilities are shared, providing insights into the task allocations and synergies that contribute to the successful creation of ML-based solutions. To answer *RQ1*, we evaluated the participation of software engineers and data scientists in multiple stages of the ML-enabled

Table 1. Case Study Goal

Analyze	the interaction between software engineers and data scientists
for the purpose of	characterization
with respect to	responsibility sharing and collaboration
from the point of view of	experienced software engineers and data scientists
in the context of	a large ML-enabled system project for Online Dispute Resolution (ODR) to help settle legal disputes.

system's creation, such as during the system's design and model development. For each activity, we mapped the actors and if any collaboration happened.

RQ2: How do software engineers and data scientists collaborate when developing an ML-enabled system?

This question focuses on the collaboration between software engineers and data scientists during the development of ML-enabled systems. It seeks to uncover the nature of their interactions, communication methods, and joint efforts, contributing to understanding the collaborative processes. To this end, we asked participants about their perceptions of how this interaction unfolded inside the team. We encouraged them to highlight challenges and improvement possibilities, which we used to formulate recommendations for other teams building ML-enabled systems.

3.2   Case and Subject Selection

The selected case concerns an Online Dispute Resolution (ODR) system project. It was created to help parties settle legal disputes in Rio de Janeiro. The system uses ML to generate settlement agreements for cases with low legal complexity, therefore avoiding litigation. We chose to focus on this particular project because it is centered around the development of an ML-enabled system, aligning with the scope of our intended investigation. Furthermore, we had easy access to project participants and the complete system documentation.

The project started in 2021 inside PUC-Rio's Tecgraf Institute through a partnership with the Rio de Janeiro State Court. After applying the Lean Inception methodology [18], the team defined the product's main functionalities. Given the system's goal, developing an ML component to aid in dispute resolution was considered an interesting choice. This led to the incorporation of data scientists into the team, which also began participating in meetings to understand business rules and discuss model characteristics. For the system's first version, the team partnered with an electric power company and established their focus on disputes involving consumer complaints directed to this company. The company representatives then developed external APIs that the system would consume to obtain all the data required by the model.

Process and Team Configuration. The project follows the Scrum framework with sprints of two weeks. Ceremonies include sprint planning, daily meetings, sprint review, and sprint retrospectives. The team responsible for developing the system is multidisciplinary. It comprises a project manager, domain experts, UX designers, data scientists, and software engineers. All team members participated in meetings to understand business rules and discuss solution ideas. Customer representatives also attended these meetings to ensure decisions followed their expectations. Besides providing requirements, they also evaluated the team's deliveries through release versions made available by the software engineers every two months. With respect to the target roles, the team comprises six software engineers and two data scientists, considered part of two separate squads. Each squad has its tasks, as well as its own planning and daily meetings. However, the teams share the same product owner.

Architecture and ML Component. Figure 1 provides an overview of the system's architecture. Users have access to the system's functionalities through a web application that communicates with back-end services through a REST API. The back-end architecture is based on microservices, with each service having a single responsibility. The services communicate both synchronously and asynchronously. Synchronous communication happens through REST APIs, while asynchronous communication occurs via message queues.

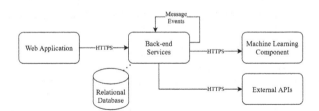

Fig. 1. Simplified System Architecture

One of the system's back-end services communicates with the ML component through a REST API. The model's input consists of data entered by users on the web system and complementary data obtained from the external APIs. As output, the model returns whether it can generate a settlement agreement. If the result is positive, the model returns all agreement parameters. If it is negative, the model returns why it could not create an agreement.

The model consists of a decision tree with a set of fixed rules, defined by customer representatives and the partner company, that must be validated before the system can generate a settlement agreement. These rules were created to restrain the model's possible outputs and improve transparency. Having verified all rules with a positive outcome, the model evaluates data from other previously resolved disputes. After selecting and analyzing the most similar disputes, the model defines the ideal value for each settlement agreement parameter, such as the value for compensating moral damages. The text classification method behind the model's functionality is described in the work of Coelho *et al.* [19].

3.3 Data Collection

We formulated our interview questions based on the work of Villamizar *et al.* [7], which offers a conceptual diagram that models tasks and related concerns typically faced by different stakeholders in ML projects. Using such diagram, we initially mapped tasks associated with the infrastructure perspective involving either a software engineer or a data scientist, presented in Table 2.

Table 2. Tasks of the Infrastructure Perspective

Task	Description
Update the Model	Involves specifying how the ML-enabled system can continuously learn from new data.
Make the Model Available	Concerns defining how the model will be consumed, e.g., through a web endpoint.
Observe the Model	Concerns determining how model performance and results will be monitored.
Store the Model	Involves defining where the ML artifacts, such as models and scripts, will be stored.
Integrate the Model	Addresses how communication between components is established to provide functionality for the ML-enabled system.

We also investigated tasks from perspectives outside the system's infrastructure, described in Table 3. We did this to have a broader view of the responsibilities of software engineers and data scientists inside the project. Given that all perspectives may instigate interaction between a data scientist and a software engineer, we designed our interview script to investigate how participants handled these tasks in the context of the project. Specifically, we had questions about (i) the interviewee's participation in each task, (ii) the interaction with a data scientist or software engineer on that task, (iii) the perceived difficulties or improvement opportunities during task execution, and (iv) the documentation originated by that task. We used this interview design to guide the discussions we had with the participants while allowing them to share their thoughts and insights freely. We recorded all interviews and, to transcribe them, we used Google Cloud's Speech-to-Text API[1].

---

[1] https://cloud.google.com/speech-to-text.

Table 3. Evaluated Perspectives

Perspective	Description
System Objectives	Involves understanding the problem to be solved by the ML-enabled system and defining the model's goals.
User Experience	Involves designing an appropriate interaction between the user and the model.
Data	Addresses how data is obtained and analyzed to build the model.
Model	Concerns defining the model's inputs and outputs and evaluating its performance.

3.4 Analysis Procedure

After acquiring all text files, we analyzed each transcription and made corrections while listening to the recordings. We also removed direct references to employee names to guarantee anonymity. The revised interview transcriptions can be found in our online open science repository[2].

For analyzing the data, we followed the guidelines for reflexive thematic analysis (RTA) defined by Braun and Clarke [5,6]. Although RTA is widely used in psychology research, studies have shown that it can be applied in other fields, such as software engineering [20] and human-computer interaction [21]. We decided to use RTA in our research since it allows us to engage analytically with the data. In other types of TA methodologies, such as coding reliability approaches, the analysis provides summaries of what was said about a particular topic [22]. In our case, we were interested in finding and interpreting patterns inside the data to fully understand the scenario illustrated by our participants and extract the main challenges they reported. Following the recommendations of Brown and Clarke [22], we did not consider using grounded theory due to the small size of our sample and the fact we do not have the goal of developing a theory.

The first phase of RTA is to familiarize with the data, which we did while reviewing the transcriptions and listening to the recordings. After that, we started the coding process. With this process, we aim to group together different data components so that all information covering a given topic is in the same category. To do this, we first read each transcript thoroughly. Then, for each relevant text fragment, we create a code. As we keep reading, we either assign more sentences to one of the codes or create a new one. We followed an inductive approach for coding, where codes are developed using the data itself as a starting point.

With the codes defined, we grouped them into themes. To find them, we looked for similarities between the codes. Themes should be objective and underpinned by a central concept. They must contain useful information about the

---

[2] https://doi.org/10.5281/zenodo.10035304.

dataset, directly addressing at least one research question. Following RTA recommendations, we iteratively refined the themes until they met these criteria.

4   Case Study Results

4.1   Participant Characterization

The participants verbally agreed to participate voluntarily in the study and have their interviews recorded. All subjects identified as male and hold a master's or a doctorate degree. Table 4 shows the roles, education level, and years of work experience for each one.

Table 4. Demographic Data about the Respondents

Participant ID	Role	Education Level	Years of Experience
DS1	Data Scientist	Doctorate	8
DS2	Data Scientist	Doctorate	8
SE1	Software Engineer	Masters degree	11
SE2	Software Engineer	Masters degree	12

4.2   Results

We summarized our findings into five main categories: **requirements, planning, data management, model management,** and **team interaction.** We included direct quotes and paraphrased statements from the practitioners to support the analysis and interpretations.

Requirements. An overview of the case study findings related to requirements can be seen in Fig. 2. An explanation for each one follows.

Managing the requirements for the ML-enabled system was a challenge. Participants emphasized that requirements constantly changed. DS1 provided an example: "*In the beginning, we had defined that the model would be as flexible as possible. We realized during later meetings this would not be well accepted, as it would make the model's results less predictable.*"

Customer representatives helped to define requirements for the model. SE1 gave examples of their participation: "*I noticed that customer representatives could actively suggest model parameter adjustments. Another topic they discussed was keeping information about the model's operation private from end users. This was done to prevent them from learning how to manipulate the model in their favor.*" DS2 also recognized the importance of customer involvement, mentioning that he felt like customer representatives could have participated more: "*We had difficulties because we did not include more customer*

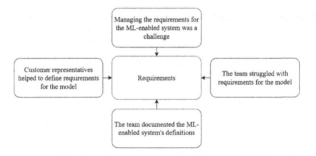

Fig. 2. Findings for the Requirements category

representatives when we defined the product's concepts. They could have helped us by making decisions. Instead, we made decisions internally. We had to revisit some of these decisions later, while we were lucky not to in others."

The team struggled with requirements for the model. Data scientists mentioned that model requirements were unrealistic and unclear at the beginning of the project. DS2 stated: *"The requirements were abstract, like 'the model needs to be fast' or 'the system needs to be easy to use.' There was a misalignment between what was desired and what was possible, which led to many meetings."*

The team documented the ML-enabled system's definitions and recognized the importance of doing so. DS2 explained: *"Each model definition was documented through presentations we did in meetings to showcase what our team was proposing. The architecture of the model was also described in a document."* DS1 highlighted the importance of documenting each meeting: *"We created a flowchart with all the rules the model considered and documented the meetings through minutes. We even had an episode where it was necessary to resort to these minutes to prove that the team had made certain decisions in a previous encounter."* DS1 also mentioned how these documents helped him learn about the project when joining the team: *"Reports were developed at the beginning of the project [...]. These documents helped me understand the business faster."*

Planning. An overview of the findings related to planning is provided in Fig. 3. An explanation of the results that emerged from the analysis follows.

Fig. 3. Findings for the Planning category

Data scientists performed activities out of their field of expertise, such as eliciting requirements for the system. DS2 explained: *"Our team was responsible for understanding the entire business flow and legal procedures so that we could build the model. Someone else could have done this survey and delivered the requirements to us."* The data science team also developed the model consumption API. In DS2's view, this should have been done by the software engineers: *"We were a research team, not a development team. Still, we needed to develop versions and generate specifications for the model. Our team was responsible for developing and maintaining the model consumption API. This responsibility could have been given to the software engineering team."*

Software engineers and data scientists struggled when planning their tasks; they tried to plan their activities separately, only communicating when necessary. SE2 explained this process: *"We created a REST API to allow the model integration with the system. We defined a communication interface for the API, and then each team did its part. It was outside the data science team's interest to understand how we stored the data as long as this service existed."*. Nevertheless, some participants were unhappy with this decision, especially with the coordination between the two teams. Each team had its own goals for each sprint, and dependencies between them were not always correctly mapped. DS2 stated: *"There was a misalignment in planning regarding each team's dependencies. For example, software engineers sometimes depended on a change in the model that was not in our backlog. The roles of each team ended up not being clear, which led to problems in the API used to consume the model. We lacked comprehensive planning that involved both teams more."*

Data Management. The findings that emerged from the qualitative analysis related to data management are shown in Fig. 4.

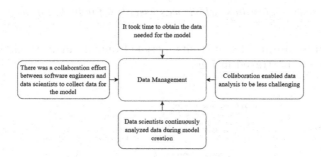

Fig. 4. Findings for the Data Management category

It took time to obtain the data needed for the model. DS2 described how this situation led to undesired development tasks: *"We also had problems with data availability. It took us some months to get all the valid data needed* *for testing. Therefore, we had to initially use mocked data, which later became different from the real data, leading to rework."*

There was a collaboration effort between software engineers and data scientists to collect data for the model. All participants confirmed the data science team was responsible for analyzing and documenting the data, and no software engineer participated in these activities. Even though software engineers did not directly analyze data, they collaborated with data scientists on other tasks. They were responsible for obtaining the data from customer representatives and making it available to the data science team, as explained by DS1: *"Since we worked with legal processes containing sensitive data, we needed a secure way to obtain them. The development team defined how this would be done together with customer representatives. They created a tool to download the data and make it available on our server."*

Data scientists continuously analyzed data during model creation. Both data scientists agreed that the analysis was not trivial. DS2 explained: *"Pre-processing the data was complex. We received raw data, so cleaning procedures were necessary, and we also put a lot of effort into annotating the data. It took a lot of effort to analyze and process the data received so that we could work on the model. This situation also affected what algorithms we could use for the model."* Data analysis also uncovered new model input fields that needed to be included, as explained by DS1: *"[...] it took us a while to figure out what data we needed to request from the customer. We defined some data fields during development, while others were defined during meetings"*.

Collaboration enabled data analysis to be less challenging. As raw data was received in files, the software engineers created a tool to help with the analysis. DS1 explained: *"The development team helped us to create a text annotation system and make it available to the domain experts. They [the domain experts] indicated which document parameters were most interesting for extraction and annotated the data we used for model training. They were always by our side to answer questions, which was essential for building the model."*

Model Management. Results that emerged from our analysis related to model management are portrayed in Fig. 5.

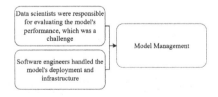

Fig. 5. Findings for the Model Management category

Data scientists were responsible for evaluating the model's performance, which was a challenge. DS1 and DS2 mentioned that it was not easy to define metrics for the model, such as a target accuracy. DS2 mentioned *"the time taken to obtain valid data hindered the time to create a better performance evaluation framework."* To solve this, the team agreed to validate the model results together with customer representatives. DS2 explained: *"We presented model studies to the project's stakeholders for them to evaluate if the results were adequate or not."* DS1 also mentioned that *"a committee of customer representatives was responsible for validating the results produced by the model.".* When asked about implementing incremental learning for the model, participants DS1 and DS2 both said this was a future goal.

Software engineers handled the model's deployment and infrastructure. SE1 stated: *"We are responsible for deploying the model consumption API. The deployment of this service [...] is automated through a CI/CD pipeline."* SE2 explained why the software engineers had this responsibility: *"We already had a pattern for deployment beforehand, and we knew the data scientists did not specialize in DevOps, so we left this structure ready for them."* Furthermore, the software engineering team developed the web application and the back-end services that consume the model.

Team Interaction. Finally, Fig. 6 presents our findings related to team interaction. Each finding is discussed below.

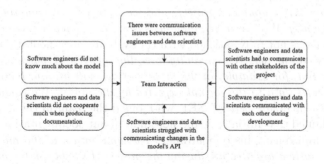

Fig. 6. Findings for the Team Interaction category

There were communication issues between software engineers and data scientists, which caused problems in the ML-enabled system. SE1 explained the discovery of errors in the data received by the model: *"I did not have the necessary knowledge to analyze if the data was correct and what fields were required or optional. Problems only appeared when we started testing. [...] If the teams had not been so distant, we could have anticipated these problems."* SE2, on the other hand, exemplified communication issues by explaining how the team should have discussed how to store the model artifacts: *"We provided Git repositories for this storage, but the teams did not discuss how the data scientists would store the artifacts. This eventually caused issues because the model had a* *lot of artifacts, such as the training scripts, which were not separated from the API code. For this reason, large files were loaded unnecessarily every time a new model release was generated."*

Software engineers did not know much about the model. Since data scientists and software engineers had different responsibilities, they became unaware of each other's activities. SE1 explained his view of this situation: *"We were very separated, and I did not like that. We did not know much about the model. It was like a 'black box' [...]. Even with a well-defined API, things that were obvious to the data science team were unclear to us. [...] We only developed the services that consumed it, so we did not know what was being done."* This situation proved to be a problem when defining the model's input, as SE1 highlighted: *"When we met with customer representatives and data scientists to map the data required by the model, I was unsure if the data we requested was correct since I did not know what the data scientists expected for the model input."*

Software engineers and data scientists did not cooperate much when producing documentation, as each team was responsible for documenting different parts of the system. DS1 explained: *"The software engineers documented the input data, while we documented the output data."* However, changes in the system harmed this process, as explained by SE2: *"Our biggest challenge was regarding the changes. The system's initial state was well-documented, but then changes started happening. These changes were not documented properly, which harmed the alignment between the teams. We did not correctly update the documentation throughout the project, and we also did not communicate these changes efficiently. We discovered them as system components stopped working."* Likewise, SE1 was not fully satisfied with the system's documentation: *"It is not documented well enough. We currently have the model's output and input data documented. But, for example, in the middle of this integration, there is a mapper that converts data to the format expected by the model. We could have documented this conversion better."* SE1, who joined the team in the middle of the project, explained that initially he did not know about documentation that could have helped him during his onboarding: *"I became aware of the model's objectives and the system architecture during the project. I would ask the data science team questions when I had doubts. There was no formal passage of knowledge but instead explanations on demand."*

Software engineers and data scientists had to communicate with other stakeholders of the project. SE2 gave an example: *"We had several discussions with customer representatives to understand their product vision and define what was possible. From there, the UX designers started to prototype ideas that we later used to model the system database"*. Data scientists also interacted with customer representatives to define requirements and explain the business rules behind the model's behavior.

Software engineers and data scientists communicated with each other during development, and we noticed how they had a good relationship inside the team. DS1 emphasized this by stating: *"We do not have any problems in terms of communication between the teams, as the software engineers are very* *attentive and available to us. When there is a change, like new data that needs to be included in the API, or when there is an issue, we communicate directly through messages."*

Software engineers and data scientists struggled with communicating changes in the model's API. SE2 stated: *"Problems in the ML-enabled system were caused by changes in the communication interface established for the API."* DS2 expressed dissatisfaction with errors in the model's input: *"Problems with input data formats when calling the model's API should not have been our responsibility, as this data had to be in the expected form before communication happened. [...] we had to build workarounds to correct input data formats, which made the system's integration with the model take time and generate rework."*

5   Discussion

5.1   How Do Software Engineers and Data Scientists Share Responsibilities When Developing an ML-Enabled System?

Data scientists and software engineers had specific responsibilities in the project. Data scientists focused on analyzing data and developing the model together with its consumption API. Software engineers, on the other hand, were responsible for the model's infrastructure and the back-end services that access it.

Both teams shared responsibilities with other project members and stakeholders. For example, they participated in meetings with customer representatives to define the ML-enabled system's goals and functionalities. Data scientists worked closely with domain experts to understand data fields and discover new ones subsequently included in the model's input. Software engineers discussed interface layouts with UX designers before implementing them on the system's web application. These findings are in line with Zhang *et al.*'s work [14], which indicates that software engineers and data scientists are present in different stages of the project, from developing the system to communicating with stakeholders.

Participants illustrated multiple interaction points between the software engineering and data science teams. They had several meetings to define model inputs and outputs and to enable model integration with the rest of the system. The same happened during data collection, when software engineers helped data scientists obtain the data for model training. Both teams also interacted during data annotation, as the software engineers created a system to help with this process. The developed tool allowed domain experts to select text areas inside the files and associate them with a data field, structuring the data for the model.

The interviews revealed that DS2 was not pleased with all the responsibilities his team received. They had to map the business flow behind processing legal disputes, elicit requirements for the model, and present ideas to stakeholders. They also had to make several decisions regarding model features; not all could be validated with customer representatives. DS2 also explained the data science team's participation in developing the model consumption API. Even though they were a research team, they developed all the API's code, a skill they did not have much experience with. For this reason, software engineers helped them during the process. Software engineers also handled the model's infrastructure and deployment pipeline since this was another skill the data scientists did not possess. Data scientists struggling with ML infrastructure was a concern mentioned in Nahar et al.'s work [16].

Team members performing activities outside their field of expertise highlights an opportunity to improve planning, which was another topic mentioned during the interviews. Participants revealed that features developed by software engineers could not be deployed because data scientists had to prioritize other functionalities. Although both teams tried to work as independently as possible, having such dependencies effectively mapped and planned could have enhanced the team's delivery speed and avoided problems during the model's integration.

5.2 How Do Software Engineers and Data Scientists Collaborate When Developing an ML-Enabled System?

Participants viewed communication between the software engineering and data science teams positively. Both teams had a good relationship and were always helpful when a member had doubts. They had a group chat where they could interact at any given time.

However, their communication could have been more efficient. Both teams worked almost independently. This reduced the frequency of interactions between them, which led to software engineers not having much knowledge about the model. Even though the model had a well-defined API, which was discussed by both teams, SE1 and SE2 used the term "black box" to describe the ML component. This lack of knowledge became evident during meetings with customer representatives, as there was a mismatch between the participants' understanding of the data. For example, one of the software engineers could not evaluate if the requested data was sufficient for the model, nor if they were in the expected format. This situation caused errors in the ML-enabled system that were only discovered during testing, resulting in avoidable rework.

Constant changes in requirements, also observed in Wan et al.'s work [23], worsened the ineffective communication between data scientists and software engineers. As new requirements appeared, the model and the system had to be updated. The data science team had to implement new data fields for the model's input and business rules for the model's output. At the same time, software engineers needed to change the system to capture such data fields, either by user input or through accessing an external API. These changes provoked errors in the system because they were not communicated properly among the teams. For this reason, data scientists had to develop adaptations in the model consumption API to accommodate different input data formats.

The team made an effort to document product definitions and the ML-enabled system architecture. Meeting decisions were registered in minutes, and data scientists and software engineers were responsible for documenting different system components. Software engineers documented the model's input data and the back-end services that consume the model. Data scientists documented the business rules behind the model's behavior and its output responses.

This separation of responsibilities made maintaining the documentation harder. New features were constantly being developed, and the team struggled with keeping documents up to date. The aforementioned inefficient communication of changes in the system was another obstacle when updating documentation. For example, problems with changes in the model's input were fixed by creating mappers that corrected the format of input data fields, and one participant mentioned that these mappers could be better documented.

Communication between the data science and software engineering teams was essential for one participant who joined the team after product development had started. SE1's understanding of the ML-enabled system's objectives and architecture was acquired through conversations and questions to the team, as no formal documentation was presented to him. The data fields used by the model are very specific to its domain, which makes understanding them difficult for someone unfamiliar with all the business rules of legal procedures.

5.3 Comparison with Literature

Our findings are consistent with results from previous studies regarding the collaboration between data scientists and software engineers developing ML-enabled systems. Many collaboration challenges discussed by Nahar *et al.* [16] were reported in our interviews, such as data scientists working isolated from software engineers, insufficient system documentation, and problems with responsibility sharing. The authors identified three collaboration points: identifying and decomposing requirements, negotiating training data quality and quantity, and integrating data science and software engineering work. All of these points were also present in our case study project. Our findings even reported a new collaboration point, where software engineers developed a system used by domain experts to help in data annotation for model training.

We could also identify several challenges illustrated by Mailach and Norbert [15]. For instance, it was clear that the software engineers did not know enough about the model, describing it as a black box. In addition, we noticed disconnections between the development team and some project stakeholders, especially when defining requirements for the model. In our research, however, the participants did not explicitly mention production delays due to these adversities.

5.4 Implications for Practitioners

Based on our findings, we present recommendations for practitioners to improve collaboration between software engineers and data scientists. We seek to aid teams developing ML-enabled systems to avoid the abovementioned pitfalls.

One of the key challenges that software engineers and data scientists face when interacting and collaborating on ML-enabled systems is the lack of clear requirements specifications. Without well-defined requirements, it can be difficult for these actors to understand each other's needs and expectations, leading to miscommunication and inefficiencies in the development process. This highlights the importance of establishing and maintaining clear requirements specifications that can serve as a shared understanding between software engineers and data scientists, enabling them to work together more efficiently.

Fostering a collaborative culture from the start of the project is fundamental. We believe this can be achieved by establishing a comprehensive planning of the system that involves all actors and stakeholders. While planning, the responsibilities of each actor must be clear to everyone on the team. Moreover, actors should be comfortable with the tasks they will perform or at least be willing to learn how to execute them. If there are any dependencies between actors that require their cooperation, these should be mapped in advance to prevent any delays during development.

Despite their background and cultural differences, software engineers and data scientists should avoid working isolated from one another. Even though some tasks can be executed independently, they need to communicate frequently. Teams should also encourage knowledge exchange between them, which can be done by pairing a member from each role to work on a task together. Another possibility is to have members of a role present their work to the rest of the team so that other actors can become familiar with their activities.

ML-enabled system architecture and definitions documentation can also enhance the interaction between these two actors. These documents should provide a concise and unambiguous description of what the ML-enabled system and each of its components should do. This facilitates the discussion between team members, who can use this documentation as a reference, preventing misconceptions. As illustrated by our results, such documentation can also be extremely useful while onboarding new team members.

5.5   Threats to Validity

This section discusses threats to validity, focusing on four types of threats: construct validity, internal validity, external validity, and reliability [4].

Construct validity refers to whether the applied research methodology is suited to answer our research questions. To mitigate threats, two of the authors had access to project documents, such as use case diagrams and system architecture documents. This documentation was used to cross-check the participants' statements. In addition, all authors revised the transcriptions, codes, and themes generated during the analysis. At the same time, the coding process in RTA is inherently subjective [6], where researchers use their own experiences while interpreting the data.

Internal validity is the extent to which our study presents truthful results for our population. To mitigate threats, we formulated the interview questions based on the findings of Villamizar *et al.* [7], which were acquired through a literature review [11] and reports of industrial experiences with ML systems [24]. We also explained the questions in detail when the participants expressed doubts to leave as little room for misunderstandings as possible. We recognize the number of participants, which was limited because of the team's size, may affect the credibility of our results. To mitigate this, we interviewed the team's most experienced software engineers and data scientists.

External validity concerns how our findings can be generalized. We understand that our case study only discussed challenges from a single team working in a specific ML-enabled system. It is possible to have scenarios where, for example, the same team is responsible for all tasks carried out by software engineers and data scientists. In other cases, a project manager might define responsibilities more formally, which can alter the team's collaboration procedures. However, given that some of our results are also present in the current literature, we believe that our case study provides additional insights that may be considered when analyzing the interaction between these two actors.

Reliability assesses to what extent the study is dependent on the specific researchers. To improve reliability, besides the peer-reviewed qualitative procedures, we uploaded the transcription of each interview to an online repository[3], enabling auditing our analyses and facilitating the replication of our study.

6   Concluding Remarks

This paper investigated the interaction between data scientists and software engineers through a case study with a team developing an industry ML-enabled system. We interviewed two experienced members of each role about their activities and collaboration practices. We used RTA to inspect the transcriptions and extract relevant data to answer our research questions. The results gave us an overview of how the team organized their tasks inside the project and the challenges data scientists and software engineers faced. These include actors being unaware of each other's activities, frequent requirement changes, unsynchronized planning, and outdated documentation of the ML-enabled system. Our study provides concrete examples of these challenges based on a case study of a real ML-enabled system development context. These challenges were also mentioned in related work employing different empirical strategies.

Understanding how the collaboration between software engineers and data scientists unfolds inside teams with different compositions and companies with other organizational structures can enhance our findings and verify the occurrence of the challenges we reported. Therefore, we invite the community to conduct additional case studies in a variety of contexts to increase external validity. Furthermore, future work could also consider expanding our study focus to collaboration with other roles, such as business stakeholders and domain experts. These actors were continuously cited during the interviews, given their importance in defining requirements and explaining the data.

---

[3] https://doi.org/10.5281/zenodo.10035304.

References

1. Sculley, D., et al.: Hidden technical debt in machine learning systems. In: Advances in Neural Information Processing Systems, vol. 28 (2015)
2. Aho, T., Sievi-Korte, O., Kilamo, T., Yaman, S., Mikkonen, T.: Demystifying data science projects: a look on the people and process of data science today. In: Morisio, M., Torchiano, M., Jedlitschka, A. (eds.) PROFES 2020. LNCS, vol. 12562, pp. 153–167. Springer, Cham (2020). https://doi.org/10.1007/978-3-030-64148-1_10
3. Lewis, G.A., Bellomo, S., Ozkaya, I.: Characterizing and detecting mismatch in machine-learning-enabled systems. In: IEEE/ACM 1st Workshop on AI Engineering-Software Engineering for AI (WAIN). IEEE, pp. 133–140 (2021)
4. Runeson, P., Host, M., Rainer, A., Regnell, B.: Case Study Research in Software Engineering: Guidelines and Examples. Wiley, Hoboken (2012)
5. Braun, V., Clarke, V.: Using thematic analysis in psychology. Qual. Res. Psychol. **3**(2), 77–101 (2006)
6. Braun, V., Clarke, V.: Reflecting on reflexive thematic analysis. Qual. Res. Sport Exerc. Health **11**(4), 589–597 (2019)
7. Villamizar, H., Kalinowski, M., Lopes, H., Mendez, D.: Identifying concerns when specifying machine learning-enabled systems: a perspective-based approach. arXiv preprint arXiv:2309.07980 (2023)
8. Kalinowski, M., Escovedo, T., Villamizar, H., Lopes, H.: Engenharia de Software para Ciência de Dados: Um guia de boas práticas com ênfase na construção de sistemas de Machine Learning em Python. Casa do Código (2023)
9. Nazir, R., Bucaioni, A., Pelliccione, P.: Architecting ML-enabled systems: challenges, best practices, and design decisions. J. Syst. Softw. **207**, 111860 (2023)
10. Ishikawa, F., Yoshioka, N.: How do engineers perceive difficulties in engineering of machine-learning systems? - questionnaire survey. In: IEEE/ACM Joint 7th International Workshop on Conducting Empirical Studies in Industry (CESI) and 6th International Workshop on Software Engineering Research and Industrial Practice (SER&IP), pp. 2–9. IEEE (2019)
11. Villamizar, H., Escovedo, T., Kalinowski, M.: Requirements engineering for machine learning: a systematic mapping study. In: 2021 47th Euromicro Conference on Software Engineering and Advanced Applications (SEAA), pp. 29–36. IEEE (2021)
12. Kim, M., Zimmermann, T., DeLine, R., Begel, A.: Data scientists in software teams: state of the art and challenges. IEEE Trans. Software Eng. **44**(11), 1024–1038 (2017)
13. Amershi, S., et al.: Software engineering for machine learning: a case study. In: 2019 IEEE/ACM 41st International Conference on Software Engineering: Software Engineering in Practice (ICSE-SEIP), pp. 291–300. IEEE (2019)
14. Zhang, A.X., Muller, M., Wang, D.: How do data science workers collaborate? Roles, workflows, and tools. Proc. ACM Hum.-Comput. Interact. 4(CSCW1), 22:1–22:23 (2020)
15. Mailach, A., Siegmund, N.: Socio-technical anti-patterns in building ML-enabled software: insights from leaders on the forefront. In: 2023 IEEE/ACM 45th International Conference on Software Engineering (ICSE), pp. 690–702. IEEE (2023)
16. Nahar, N., Zhou, S., Lewis, G., Kästner, C.: Collaboration challenges in building ML-enabled systems: communication, documentation, engineering, and process. In: Proceedings of the 44th International Conference on Software Engineering, ICSE 2022, New York, NY, USA, Association for Computing Machinery, pp. 413–425, July 2022

17. Basili, V.R., Rombach, H.D.: The tame project: towards improvement-oriented software environments. IEEE Trans. Software Eng. **14**(6), 758–773 (1988)
18. Caroli, P.: Lean Inception. Caroli. org, São Paulo (2017)
19. Coelho, G.M., et al.: Text classification in the Brazilian legal domain. In: ICEIS (1), pp. 355–363 (2022)
20. Cruzes, D.S., Dyba, T.: Recommended steps for thematic synthesis in software engineering. In: International Symposium on Empirical Software Engineering and Measurement, pp. 275–284. IEEE (2011)
21. Brown, N., Stockman, T.: Examining the use of thematic analysis as a tool for informing design of new family communication technologies. In: 27th International BCS Human Computer Interaction Conference (HCI 2013), vol. 27, pp. 1–6 (2013)
22. Braun, V., Clarke, V.: Can I use TA? Should I use TA? Should I not use TA? Comparing reflexive thematic analysis and other pattern-based qualitative analytic approaches. Couns. Psychother. Res. **21**(1), 37–47 (2021)
23. Wan, Z., Xia, X., Lo, D., Murphy, G.C.: How does machine learning change software development practices? IEEE Trans. Software Eng. **47**(9), 1857–1871 (2019)
24. Villamizar, H., Kalinowski, M., et al.: A catalogue of concerns for specifying machine learning-enabled systems. In: Workshop on Requirements Engineering (WER), pp. 1–14 (2022)

Towards Integrating Knowledge Graphs into Process-Oriented Human-AI Collaboration in Industry

Bernhard Heinzl[1]([✉]), Agastya Silvina[1], Franz Krause[2], Nicole Schwarz[1], Kabul Kurniawan[3], Elmar Kiesling[3], Mario Pichler[1], and Bernhard Moser[1]

[1] Software Competence Center Hagenberg GmbH, Hagenberg, Austria
bernhard.heinzl@scch.at
[2] University of Mannheim, Mannheim, Germany
[3] Vienna University of Economics and Business, Vienna, Austria

Abstract. Human-AI collaboration in industrial manufacturing promises to overcome current limitations by combining the flexibility of human intelligence and the scaling and processing capabilities of machine intelligence. To ensure effective collaboration between human and AI team members, we envision a software-driven coordination mechanism that orchestrates the interactions between the participants in Human-AI teaming scenarios and help to synchronize the information flow between them. A structured process-oriented approach to systems engineering aims at generalizability, deployment efficiency and enhancing the quality of the resulting software by formalizing the human-AI interaction as a BPMN process model. During runtime, this process model is executed by the teaming engine, one of the core components of the Teaming.AI software platform. By incorporating dynamic execution traces of these process models into a knowledge graph structure and linking them to contextual background knowledge, we facilitate the monitoring of variations in process executions and inference of new insights during runtime. Knowledge graphs are a powerful tool for semantic integration of diverse data, thereby significantly improving the data quality, which is still one of the biggest issues in AI-driven software solutions. We present the Teaming.AI software platform and its key components as a framework for enabling transparent teamwork between humans and AI in industry. We discuss its application in the context of an industrial use case in plastic injection molding production. Overall, this Teaming.AI platform provides a robust, flexible and accountable solution for human-AI collaboration in manufacturing.

Keywords: Industrial Knowledge Graph · Process Orchestration · Human-AI Collaboration · Plastic Injection Molding

1 Introduction

With the emergence of Industry 5.0 as a paradigm, the landscape of industrial manufacturing is evolving, representing a shift from the purely automated and machine-centric approaches towards focusing on the integration and collaboration between humans and

P. Bludau et al. (Eds.): SWQD 2024, LNBIP 505, pp. 76–87, 2024.
https://doi.org/10.1007/978-3-031-56281-5_5

advanced technologies like Artificial Intelligence (AI), Internet of Things (IoT), and robotics. Industry 5.0 emphasizes the human-centric aspect, aiming to combine the strengths of both humans and machines, while also taking into account the different and unique characteristics of its participants, to achieve higher productivity, innovation, and sustainable growth [1, 2].

In contrast to typical human-in-the-loop settings, human-AI collaboration involves teaming orchestration, i.e., monitoring and real-time management of complex activities, and addresses a broader scope of tasks [3, 4]. For example, in plastic injection molding production, human operators and AI systems can collaborate on carrying out quality inspection, predictive maintenance or deciding on process parameter optimizations.

Such teaming orchestration requires coordination mechanisms and workflows that can be implemented by means of software solutions. A structured engineering approach to systematic and process-oriented modeling of such orchestration mechanisms based on a formal description language has the potential to be generalizable and applicable across various use cases while also leading to better software quality and increased operational efficiency in the end result. However, realizing such coordination mechanisms by means of computational models is still an under-explored research challenge [5, 6].

In this context, the adoption of Business Process Model and Notation (BPMN) [7, 8] has emerged as a powerful means for managing business processes. BPMN offers a standardized and executable modeling language with an intuitive graphical notation [8]. Using BPMN, we can capture and model the dynamics of interactions between human operators and AI systems in collaborative manufacturing tasks.

The BPMN language is supported by various modeling tools as well as Business Process Management systems (BPMS). These BPMS are able to execute BPMN-based workflows and provide dynamic traces of these process execution instances during run-time. Such dynamic traces can not only serve the purpose of monitoring and auditing the activities undertaken, but also offer insights into decision-making instances, tracking, e.g., what decisions were made when and by whom, whether by humans or AI. This level of traceability is beneficial not just for auditing purposes but also for enhancing machine learning-based processing, enabling anomaly detection, and further refinement of AI systems. It also offers transparency and increases trustworthiness in AI systems.

For a more comprehensive understanding and operational enhancement, linking these dynamic process execution traces to static background knowledge becomes essential. Knowledge graphs (KGs) provide a solution for this integration by means of a graph structure consisting of nodes and edges. Industrial knowledge graphs have become essential tools in the industrial sector because they allow integration of heterogeneous data sources into a structured graph format. The potential of knowledge graphs lies in their capacity for rich semantic integration reasoning and knowledge discovery [9]. The integration of static domain and context knowledge with dynamically generated data from process executions represents a novel frontier [10], extending KGs beyond their traditional static focus. Leveraging this dynamic knowledge can significantly improve data quality, enhance decision-making during operation and pave the way for downstream applications, such as recommendation systems or deriving KG embeddings for machine learning applications [11].

As the main contribution of this paper, we present the Teaming.AI software platform that integrates BPMN process model execution for orchestration with knowledge graphs for data management and contextualization, and event-based communication with AI systems. We also discuss its application to a plastic injection molding use case. This work is part of the Teaming.AI[1] research project, where we aim towards improving human-AI collaboration in industrial manufacturing and realizing the vision of more seamless, adaptive and efficient collaboration of humans and AI systems in modern industrial AI-based applications in the context of Industry 5.0.

2   Related Work

In the context of enhancing process modeling with semantic web technologies, ontologies such as [12–16] have emerged that formalize BPMN concepts. For example, the BPMN Based Ontology (BBO) [12] defines a set of concepts and properties to capture BPMN concepts like activities, events, gateways, or sequence flows. Based on this BBO ontology, tools like BPMN2KG [17] allow to transform valid BPMN process diagrams into RDF-based knowledge graph representations. Ontology-based process modeling [18] aims to enhance the interoperability of BPMN systems, however, such frameworks have yet to be adopted in industrial settings, due to the significant manual effort required to develop use-case-specific BPMN ontologies [15]. The existing approaches also do not cover dynamic process instances, which limits their applicability for capturing process executions [10].

Numerous recent works investigate human-robot collaboration in smart manufacturing settings. For example, Othman and Yang [19] conducted a systemic review of the key technologies currently being employed in smart manufacturing with human-robot collaboration systems. Feddoul et al. [20] highlighted the increasing overlap between digital twins and human-robot interactions in industrial settings. While these works do promote collaboration between operators and automated systems in manufacturing environments, they focus more on the physical interactions and hardware aspects between humans and robots, whereas we are more concerned with the cognitive and social aspects of collaboration, such as mutual understanding, communication, coordination, and trust [21].

Knowledge graphs have been widely recognized as an important technology in AI and have been extensively used for data management. Wang & Chen [22] discussed the state-of-the-art research on knowledge graph data management, including knowledge graph data models, query languages, storage schemes, query processing, and reasoning. In [23], the authors present a characterization of different types of knowledge graphs along with their construction approaches.

In [24], the authors explore how process modeling and mining can benefit from the use of knowledge graphs and machine learning techniques, in particular in the context of business processes. The paper discusses enterprise KGs and temporal KGs, their applications and relevance for process mining. The paper also reviews BPMN, surveys existing approaches for integrating process models with knowledge graphs and presents

---

[1] https://www.teamingai-project.eu/.

various machine learning methods that can be applied to process modeling and mining, such as graph embedding, graph neural networks, and deep learning. In contrast, our approach aims to integrate human-AI collaboration, where AI models serve to aid human tasks in industrial manufacturing rather than employing AI on top of KGs for mining existing process executions.

Our work builds upon the existing body of research in human-AI collaboration, knowledge graphs, and process modeling. By integrating these technologies, we present a comprehensive software platform that supports human-AI teamwork collaboration in industrial manufacturing.

3   Process Modeling and Orchestration

The orchestration of collaborative tasks between humans and AI involves monitoring, managing in real-time, and ensuring seamless coordination. Rather than treating AI systems as mere substitutes for humans, effective team orchestration aims to combine their respective strengths to overcome current limitations in high-complexity collaborative tasks while at the same time respecting the distinct characteristics of each entity involved [6].

To achieve this, orchestration needs to follow a structured and generalizable approach applicable across various use cases and domains. On the one hand, it requires clear rules to determine, for example, when to request data labels from a human operator, or which samples to choose intelligently to be most effective. AI systems should guide humans and make appropriate queries to obtain the desired information. At the same time, it is important to efficiently manage and use the managed data, both labeled and unlabeled, to improve and evolve an AI system over time. On the other hand, implementing these rules in software necessitates a generalizable approach that allows the creation of workflow pipelines without modifying the software code extensively when adopting the software platform to a new use case or refining existing deployments [25].

To address these challenges, we pursue a model-based approach that enables the specification of teaming workflows and human-AI interaction patterns through process models. These process models allow to change communication patterns and sequences by means of model configuration, ensuring adaptability and maintainability in large-scale scenarios.

However, to fully capture the dynamics of real-world teaming processes, a single static process model is usually not sufficient. Instead, we must consider alternative pathways, dynamic switches, and variations in execution, such as role sharing. Therefore, we need to combine process models with dynamic information modeling that captures runtime dynamics in process executions.

Process models allow the formal definition of human-AI teaming processes by describing the structure of the process and then assigning individual tasks to agents (human or AI) that perform the assigned task. Dedicated language for modeling business processes, such as BPMN [26], can also be adopted in manufacturing scenarios [27, 28]. As an example, Fig. 1 below depicts an illustrative BPMN process model for a plastic injection molding use case, similar to the one described in Sect. 6.

During the initialization phase, software engineers and domain experts instantiate and tailor these process models for the specific use case. These models can be linked to other

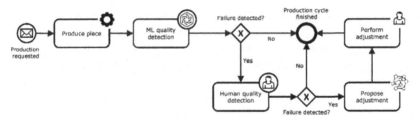

Fig. 1. Simplified BPMN process model for a manufacturing task involving quality inspection and parameter adjustment.

rules and knowledge captured in the knowledge graph (see also Sect. 4), encompassing, for example, legal or ethics policies governing data privacy, employee conduct, and algorithmic decision-making standards.

For executing the process models at runtime, we leverage state-of-the-art technology, in particular Camunda and Apache Kafka to help in process automation and facilitate synchronizing the information flow. More details on the implementation are given in Sect. 5.

4   Dynamic Knowledge Graph

Knowledge graphs are a powerful tool for knowledge modeling, by providing a comprehensive and interconnected view on knowledge and information. Knowledge graphs enable effective organization, retrieval, reasoning, and discovery of knowledge within industrial production settings. They allow to capture rich semantic relationships between entities in complex graph-based knowledge structures [25]. They facilitate a systematic approach to knowledge modeling and integration, allowing for the conceptualization and management of diverse knowledge types. This capability becomes pivotal in supporting real-time decision-making.

To ensure manageability and scalability, it is important to adopt a strategic approach for incorporating data into the KG. Instead of including all available data, it is preferable to facilitate an approach driven by use case requirements. For instance, it might be beneficial to include domain knowledge that help to contextualize other data or observational knowledge and events that might affect the execution flow in the process model. On the other hand, e.g., collections of large-scale structured measurement data might be managed more efficiently in relational database systems or data lakes instead. For such data, a KG may act as a data catalog that facilitates semantic localization of source data [29]. Incorporating knowledge graph schemas, such as ontologies, adds another layer by allowing to validate data consistency within the graph.

While knowledge graphs usually focus on representing static information, they also allow to capture dynamic knowledge, in particular process model execution traces. Linking these traces to existing domain background knowledge within an industrial KG enriches the comprehension of operational intricacies and enables to gain a better understanding of their operations. Such linked background knowledge might include, e.g., skills and credentials of human operators, based on which policies might be set in place about which operator might be tasked with making certain decision.

Leveraging this information within the KG allows not only for informed decision-making but also for auditable process monitoring, where auditors are able to retrieve information about which decision was made by which entity. Especially in human-AI collaborative tasks, these insights may be used to monitor the performance of AI models and notify in case of declining model accuracy signaled by increased discrepancies between AI predictions and human input. As a consequence, a specific task might be reassigned from AI models to human operators when necessary, ensuring optimal performance aligned with predefined policies [21].

The integration of historic records of executed process instances from BPMN models into the KG offers a comprehensive record of process executions over time. This creates a semantically organized "digital shadow" that mirrors the evolution of processes and production settings. By integrating manufacturing data and contextual knowledge within the KG, this dynamic representation encompasses the ongoing and historical facets of operations at scale. Consequently, users gain not only insight into current operations but also a detailed view of their evolution over time, providing a holistic perspective on operations and offering support for more comprehensive decision-making [10].

5 Teaming.AI Platform

This section provides an overview of the Teaming.AI platform implementation, encompassing the components, functionalities, and utility of the system. Designed as a comprehensive software platform, it integrates benefits of AI systems with human capabilities to harness human adaptability and AI processing capacities. Figure 2 presents the Teaming.AI platform architecture and its different components.

The software architecture follows an event-driven communication paradigm, where process workflows are triggered by events. This allows for loose coupling between components and the ability to scale platform processes independently.

Playing a pivotal role in system task orchestration, the Teaming Engine Layer comprises multiple integral components. Central to this layer is the Orchestration Engine using Camunda [30] that serves as the system's core, automating tasks and coordinating their execution in a structured manner. This engine provides a mechanism for process orchestration based on BPMN workflows, ensuring that all activities are conducted in harmony and promoting operational efficiency within the Teaming.AI platform.

The Teaming.AI platform also accommodates the knowledge engine, housing a knowledge graph that maps relationships among diverse information pieces, fostering better decision-making and an improved user experience through complex data visualization. Leveraging graph-based data structures, the knowledge graph stores entity relationships, offering contextually relevant insights and information management. Continuously monitoring the knowledge graph and its dynamic updates, the knowledge engine ensures platform alignment with the current application system and teaming workflows. This ongoing overview captures updates and changes from all other components, integrating them into the knowledge graph for a constantly updated system.

Additionally, Apache Kafka [31], an open-source stream-processing software, facilitates real-time data processing of high-volume data streams. This event stream broker allows for easy data ingestion, processing, integration across systems. By using Kafka

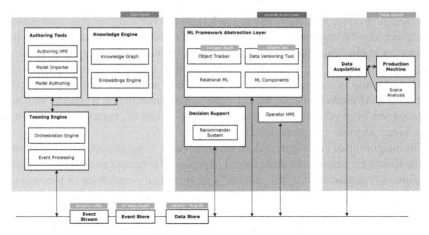

Fig. 2. Teaming.AI platform architecture

event streams, the teaming platform can monitor streams of data from various sources and process them in real time. The processed data can then be used to feed machine learning models or inform decisions within BPMN workflows. AI models can be integrated into BPMN workflows by exposing them as service endpoints. These models can then be used to make predictions or recommendations based on real-time data processing by Kafka.

Furthermore, the Framework Abstraction Layer streamlines development by providing a standardized interface for AI systems to underlying software or hardware resources. By abstracting resource complexity, developers can focus on application development without delving into underlying system intricacies. This abstraction layer triggers data analysis and AI model operations.

A use-case-specific operator HMI provides a human-centric interface to human operators and technicians during production operation (see Fig. 5 for an example). This is separate from the authoring tools (that are part of the core platform) used by software engineers and domain experts to set up, configure and maintain the platform.

6 Use Case

The following describes an application case concerning plastic injection molding that illustrates human-AI collaboration in the manufacturing domain. Figure 3 shows an overview of the use case. More details may also be found in [25].

Plastic injection molding comprises the setup of the injection process, the production of a piece and the subsequent quality inspection. In the case of defective workpieces, process parameters need to be adjusted in order to mitigate these defects. In this use case, produced pieces can either be checked automatically using ML-based visual classification, or manually double-checked by a human operator in case the AI system detects a defect or is unsure.

Once a defect has been confirmed, a human technician (process engineer) is asked to perform adjustments of machine parameters. To this end, domain knowledge about

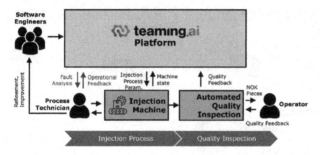

Fig. 3. Teaming.AI platform use case from plastic injection molding.

product failure types and machine parameter adjustments is queried from the KG with contextual information in order to provide decision-support.

Software engineers and domain experts are able to continuously refine and improve the operation by fine-tuning the process model, expanding the contents of the knowledge graph and calibrating AI models with new training data. Figure 4 depicts the BPMN process model that models the workflow described.

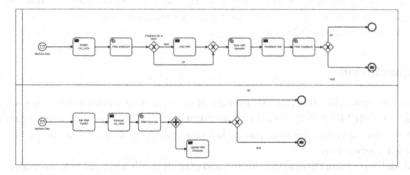

Fig. 4. BPMN model for the use case, showing the quality prediction and operator feedback.

Moreover, Fig. 5 shows screenshots of the operator HMI, where human operators and technicians are able to provide feedback regarding quality inspection (e.g., types of defects) as well as receive alerts, information about current process states or suggested parameter adjustments.

This is an example of human and AI systems working together. ML-based quality inspection supports repetitive tasks and reduces the workload for the human, while human intervention in untypical scenarios ensures adaptability and accuracy in handling exceptional or unexpected situations that require nuanced judgment.

The integration of process knowledge, real-time production data as well as domain expertise that captures diagnosis and resolving quality issues enables valuable insights into dynamic process improvements. For example, it allows to query which combinations of AI agent and human operator disagree in their quality inspection, potentially indicating a problem in the process or decreasing performance of the ML model classification

Fig. 5. HMI for the human operator giving feedback for quality inspection (left) and receiving information about the process status (right).

[10]. This allows to monitor ML model performance during runtime, which is important in all AI-based applications. It also facilitates auditability of historical process executions in order to analyze and review past operations, ensuring compliance with quality standards, identifying potential inefficiencies, and enabling continuous improvement in manufacturing processes based on insights gained from past executions.

Other use cases have been investigated as well, e.g., orchestrating manual set-up and operation of a milling machine for large-part manufacturing. For a more detailed description, we refer to [32, 33].

7   Conclusion

We have presented the Teaming.AI software platform that integrates dynamic knowledge graphs with BPMN-based workflow orchestration in order to realize more seamless, adaptive and efficient collaboration of humans and AI systems in modern industrial AI-based applications.

Model-based workflow orchestration and execution allows to capture human-AI collaborative workflows. This approach brings flexibility to process execution by allowing to apply the Teaming.AI platform to difference use cases by means of configuring process models. The BPMN language offers a domain-specific modeling language suitable for efficient and lightweight teaming model development by different domain experts. However, instead of coordinating all software communication within the platform, the Teaming Engine should focus on orchestrating interactions with humans so as to avoid teaming engine becoming a performance bottleneck.

It is important to establish connections between dynamic process data and static knowledge by means of a dynamic knowledge graph. In the use case, this integration enables to query historic process instances regarding updated failure statistics and mitigation strategies. It also enables to audit production operation retrospectively to provide transparency and increase trust in novel AI-based systems. The knowledge graph becomes a digital shadow of the production system, incorporating real-time data as well as domain knowledge and human-AI interactions.

Future work will focus on expanding the Teaming.AI platform, the integration of extended background knowledge into the knowledge graph to facilitate novel machine learning applications and knowledge inference as well as better integration of authoring tools to improve systems engineering. We also aim for novel application scenarios to different use cases in order to better explore the possibilities and limitations of this approach.

References

1. Leng, J., et al.: Industry 5.0: prospect and retrospect. J. Manuf. Syst. **65**, 279–295 (2022). https://doi.org/10.1016/j.jmsy.2022.09.017
2. Demir, K.A., Döven, G., Sezen, B.: Industry 5.0 and human-robot co-working. Procedia Comput. Sci. **158**, 688–695 (2019). https://doi.org/10.1016/j.procs.2019.09.104
3. Yang, K.B., et al.: Pair-up: prototyping human-AI co-orchestration of dynamic transitions between individual and collaborative learning in the classroom. In: Proceedings of the 2023 CHI Conference on Human Factors in Computing Systems, pp. 1–17. Association for Computing Machinery, New York, NY, USA (2023). https://doi.org/10.1145/3544548.358 1398
4. du Boulay, B., Mitrovic, A., Yacef, K.: Handbook of Artificial Intelligence in Education. Edward Elgar Publishing (2023)
5. Bansal, G., Nushi, B., Kamar, E., Lasecki, W.S., Weld, D.S., Horvitz, E.: Beyond accuracy: the role of mental models in human-AI team performance. In: Proceedings of the AAAI Conference on Human Computation and Crowdsourcing, pp. 2–11 (2019)
6. Zhang, R., McNeese, N.J., Freeman, G., Musick, G.: "An Ideal Human": expectations of AI teammates in human-AI teaming. Proc. ACM Hum.-Comput. Interact. **4**(246), 1–246:25 (2021). https://doi.org/10.1145/3432945
7. Object Management Group: Business Process Model and Notation (BPMN): Version 2.0. OMG (2011)
8. Allweyer, T.: BPMN 2.0: Introduction to the Standard for Business Process Modeling. BoD – Books on Demand (2016)
9. Hogan, A., et al.: Knowledge graphs. ACM Comput. Surv. **54** 71:1–71:37 (2021). https://doi. org/10.1145/3447772
10. Krause, F., Kurniawan, K., Kiesling, E., Paulheim, H., Polleres, A.: On the representation of dynamic BPMN process executions in knowledge graphs. In: Ortiz-Rodriguez, F., Villazón-Terrazas, B., Tiwari, S., Bobed, C. (eds.) Knowledge Graphs and Semantic Web, pp. 97–105. Springer, Cham (2023). https://doi.org/10.1007/978-3-031-47745-4_8
11. Dai, Y., Wang, S., Xiong, N.N., Guo, W.: A survey on knowledge graph embedding: approaches, applications and benchmarks. Electronics **9**, 750 (2020). https://doi.org/10.3390/ electronics9050750
12. Annane, A., Aussenac-Gilles, N., Kamel, M.: BBO: BPMN 2.0 based ontology for business process representation. In: Proceedings of the 20th European Conference on Knowledge Management. ACPI (2019). https://doi.org/10.34190/KM.19.113
13. Natschläger, C.: Towards a BPMN 2.0 ontology. In: Dijkman, R., Hofstetter, J., Koehler, J. (eds.) Business Process Model and Notation, vol. 95, pp. 1–15. Springer, Heidelberg (2011). https://doi.org/10.1007/978-3-642-25160-3_1
14. Di Martino, B., Esposito, A., Nacchia, S., Maisto, S.A.: Semantic annotation of BPMN: current approaches and new methodologies. In: Proceedings of the 17th International Conference on Information Integration and Web-Based Applications & Services, pp. 1–5. Association for Computing Machinery, New York, NY, USA (2015). https://doi.org/10.1145/2837185.283 7257

15. Corea, C., Fellmann, M., Delfmann, P.: Ontology-based process modelling - will we live to see it? In: Ghose, A., Horkoff, J., Silva Souza, V.E., Parsons, J., Evermann, J. (eds.) Conceptual Modeling, pp. 36–46. Springer, Cham (2021). https://doi.org/10.1007/978-3-030-89022-3_4

16. Rospocher, M., Ghidini, C., Serafini, L.: An ontology for the business process modelling notation. In: Formal Ontology in Information Systems-Proceedings of the Eighth International Conference, FOIS2014, 22–25 September 2014, Rio de Janeiro, Brazil, pp. 133–146. IOS Press (2014)

17. Bachhofner, S., Kiesling, E., Revoredo, K., Waibel, P., Polleres, A.: Automated process knowledge graph construction from BPMN models. In: Strauss, C., Cuzzocrea, A., Kotsis, G., Tjoa, A.M., Khalil, I. (eds.) Database and Expert Systems Applications, vol. 13426, pp. 32–47. Springer, Cham (2022). https://doi.org/10.1007/978-3-031-12423-5_3

18. Thomas, O., Fellmann M.A.M.: Semantic process modeling – design and implementation of an ontology-based representation of business processes. Bus. Inf. Syst. Eng. 1, 438–451 (2009). https://doi.org/10.1007/s12599-009-0078-8

19. Othman, U., Yang, E.: Human-robot collaborations in smart manufacturing environments: review and outlook. Sensors 23, 5663 (2023). https://doi.org/10.3390/s23125663

20. Feddoul, Y., Ragot, N., Duval, F., Havard, V., Baudry, D., Assila, A.: Exploring human-machine collaboration in industry: a systematic literature review of digital twin and robotics interfaced with extended reality technologies. Int. J. Adv. Manuf. Technol. 129, 1917–1932 (2023). https://doi.org/10.1007/s00170-023-12291-3

21. Hoch, T., et al.: Teaming.AI: enabling human-AI teaming intelligence in manufacturing. In: Proceedings of Interoperability for Enterprise Systems and Applications Workshops Co-Located with 11th International Conference on Interoperability for Enterprise Systems and Applications (I-ESA 2022), Valencia, Spain (2022)

22. Wang, X., Chen, W.: Knowledge graph data management: models, methods, and systems. In: Leong Hou, U., Yang, J., Cai, Y., Karlapalem, K., Liu, A., Huang, X. (eds.) Web Information Systems Engineering, vol. 1155, pp. 3–12. Springer, Singapore (2020). https://doi.org/10.1007/978-981-15-3281-8_1

23. Tiwari, S., Al-Aswadi, F.N., Gaurav, D.: Recent trends in knowledge graphs: theory and practice. Soft. Comput. 25, 8337–8355 (2021). https://doi.org/10.1007/s00500-021-05756-8

24. Miller, J.A., Mahmud, R.: Research directions in process modeling and mining using knowledge graphs and machine learning. In: Qingyang, W., Zhang, L.-J. (eds.) Services Computing – SCC 2022, vol. 13738, pp. 86–100. Springer, Cham (2022). https://doi.org/10.1007/978-3-031-23515-3_7

25. Krause, F., et al.: Managing human-AI collaborations within industry 5.0 scenarios via knowledge graphs: key challenges and lessons learned. Frontiers Artif. Intell., 1–30 (2023)

26. Aagesen, G., Krogstie, J.: BPMN 2.0 for modeling business processes. In: vom Brocke, J., Rosemann, M. (eds.) Handbook on Business Process Management 1: Introduction, Methods, and Information Systems, pp. 219–250. Springer, Heidelberg (2015). https://doi.org/10.1007/978-3-642-45100-3_10

27. Prades, L., Romero, F., Estruch, A., García-Dominguez, A., Serrano, J.: Defining a methodology to design and implement business process models in BPMN according to the standard ANSI/ISA-95 in a manufacturing enterprise. Procedia Eng. 63, 115–122 (2013). https://doi.org/10.1016/j.proeng.2013.08.283

28. Erasmus, J., Vanderfeesten, I., Traganos, K., Grefen, P.: Using business process models for the specification of manufacturing operations. Comput. Ind. 123, 103297 (2020). https://doi.org/10.1016/j.compind.2020.103297

29. Dibowski, H., Schmid, S., Svetashova, Y., Henson, C., Tran, T.: Using semantic technologies to manage a data lake: data catalog, provenance and access control (2020)

30. Camunda Services GmbH: The Camunda BPM Manual (2021). https://docs.camunda.org/manual/7.7/

31. Garg, N.: Apache Kafka. Packt Publishing Birmingham, UK (2013)
32. Pérez, A.A., Estrada-Lugo, H.D., Fernández, E.M.-E., Leva, M.C., Aperribai, J., Aranburu, A.: Modifying a manufacturing task for teamwork between humans and AI: initial data collection to guide requirements specifications. In: Proceedings of the 32nd European Safety and Reliability Conference (ESREL 2022), Dublin, Ireland (2022)
33. Haindl, P., Hoch, T., Dominguez, J., Aperribai, J., Ure, N.K., Tunçel, M.: Quality characteristics of a software platform for human-AI teaming in smart manufacturing. In: Vallecillo, A., Visser, J., Pérez-Castillo, R. (eds.) Quality of Information and Communications Technology, pp. 3–17. Springer, Cham (2022). https://doi.org/10.1007/978-3-031-14179-9_1

Artificial Intelligence

Impact of Image Data Splitting on the Performance of Automotive Perception Systems

Md. Abu Ahammed Babu[1,2]([✉]) [iD], Sushant Kumar Pandey[2] [iD],
Darko Durisic[1] [iD], Ashok Chaitanya Koppisetty[1], and Miroslaw Staron[2] [iD]

[1] Research & Development, Volvo Car Corporation, Gothenburg, Sweden
{darko.durisic,ashok.chaitanya.koppisetty}@volvocars.com
[2] Chalmers | University of Gothenburg, Gothenburg, Sweden
md.abu.ahammed.babu@volvocars.com,
{sushant.kumar.pandey,miroslaw.staron}@gu.se

Abstract. Context: Training image recognition systems is one of the crucial elements of the AI Engineering process in general and for automotive systems in particular. The quality of data and the training process can have a profound impact on the quality, performance, and safety of automotive software. **Objective:** Splitting data between train and test sets is one of the crucial elements in this process as it can determine both how well the system learns and generalizes to new data. Typical data splits take into consideration either randomness or timeliness of data points. However, in image recognition systems, the similarity of images is of equal importance. **Methods:** In this computational experiment, we study the impact of six data-splitting techniques. We use an industrial dataset with high-definition color images of driving sequences to train a YOLOv7 network. **Results:** The mean average precision (mAP) was 0.943 and 0.841 when the similarity-based and the frame-based splitting techniques were applied, respectively. However, the object-based splitting technique produces the worst mAP score (0.118). **Conclusion:** There are significant differences in the performance of object detection methods when applying different data-splitting techniques. The most positive results are the random selections, whereas the most objective ones are splits based on sequences that represent different geographical locations.

Keywords: Data splitting technique · Object detection · YOLOv7 · Image perception system · Autonomous driving

1 Introduction

Autonomous Driving (AD) software is usually constructed by combining multiple perception and decision sub-systems [11]. The autonomous perception sub-systems detect (perceive) objects surrounding the vehicle by using data from the operational design domain (ODD) using sensors like LiDAR [20], radar, camera,

P. Bludau et al. (Eds.): SWQD 2024, LNBIP 505, pp. 91–111, 2024.
https://doi.org/10.1007/978-3-031-56281-5_6

and ultrasound. The camera is used in object detection scenarios in autonomous driving, but today it is complemented by other signals from radar and LiDAR to ensure the safety of the decisions in autonomous driving [7]. Its usage scenarios include the identification of potential hazards in the surrounding traffic, and the detection of traffic lights, signs, and road conditions. All of the above scenarios rely on accurate object detection, which can be used in the decision sub-systems [18].

Modern object detection techniques evolved fast since the introduction of deep neural networks (DNN), in particular convolutional neural networks (CNN) and Autoencoders. The deep learning (DL) object detectors [19] use supervised or semi-supervised learning where the model learns from training images and is evaluated through various performance metrics (e.g., mean average precision (mAP)) on testing images. The effectiveness of the training process has a direct impact on the quality of the resulting model and thus the entire AD system – insufficiently trained model misclassifies objects and can be a cause of dangerous situations.

Data splitting is an important part of the process of training the model, as it determines whether the model is trained on data that is representative of the population and that the degree of similarity between data points reflects the population. In the realm of computer vision and automotive perception systems, the emphasis on data splitting surpasses the significance of data quality for several compelling reasons. The effectiveness of training models for object detection and decision-making in autonomous driving heavily relies on the distribution and diversity of the data. Data splitting, which involves partitioning the dataset into training and testing sets, plays a pivotal role in ensuring that the model can generalize well to new, unseen data. While data quality is undoubtedly crucial, especially in capturing real-world nuances, it is the strategic partitioning of data that determines how well the model extrapolates insights from the training set to make informed decisions in diverse scenarios. In the context of automotive perception systems, where accurate and timely detection of objects is paramount for safety, a carefully designed data splitting strategy becomes the linchpin for training models that can robustly navigate the complexities of real-world driving environments. Although it is a straightforward task to split the data randomly or based on the timeliness of the data points, it does not guarantee that the data is not leaked [22] from the train to the test set. In particular, in image data, two images may be different, but they can represent the same place, the same time, the same situation. This kind of information leak needs to be taken into consideration when splitting the data.

An empirical case study on the impact of data splitting strategies in the context of large-scale software systems showed that choosing random split may introduce data leakage [15]. The authors also suggested to use time-based split to significantly reduce data leakage in the context of AIOps (AI for IT operations). However, there case study is limited to one particular dataset of AIOps and the investigation is limited to only two kinds of data splittings: random split and time-based split. In this paper, we investigate the impact of different data-splitting techniques on the performance of an image recognition model. We explore six different splits: two sequence-based splits (where we ensure that images from similar driving scenarios are not part of both training and testing datasets), one time-based split (where chances of data leakage is high due to similarity of consecutive image frames), one object-based split (which is intentionally made biased), one image similarity and one image dissimilarity-based split. These splits represent the most common scenarios used in training image perception systems in general. This study finds the answer to the following research question:

RQ: *Is there a statistically significant difference in object detection model performance for different data splitting techniques?*

To answer the above question, a newly released dataset from Volvo Cars called Cirrus [24] is used in this study. Cirrus contains images from multiple real-driving scenarios. Six different data splitting techniques were applied and the results were analyzed to find whether the results are significantly different or not.

Our results show that the mean average precision (mAP) for both validation and test sets differ, and the difference is statistically significant. Among the six splits, the similarity-based split and frame-based split showed the highest performance in terms of the mean average precision while the object-based splits showed the smallest mean average precision. The replication package of the study is made available[1].

The rest of the paper is organized in the following manner. Section 2 discusses several existing research works focusing on various data-splitting strategies from different field perspectives. Section 3 provides the description of the experiment design including details of the six data splits, the chosen object detection model, and the experimental setup. Section 4 contains the results from the evaluation of the six data-splitting strategies and the statistical analysis, followed by the discussion of the findings presented in Sect. 5. Finally, threats to validity are discussed in Sect. 6 and the conclusion is drawn in Sect. 7.

2   Background and Related Work

Autonomous driving systems have always been a big concern in the transportation world. In recent years, we have seen a lot of progress in this field, thanks to Computer Vision (CV) technology. One crucial aspect of CV is object detection, which helps identify road users like vehicles, pedestrians, and also traffic lights, and traffic signs. Object detection also became the most challenging task in the context of AD systems due to the complex nature of traffic scenarios [2].

In order to train an object detection model, data needs to be split into two sets: one to expose to the model during training, the other is preserved to evaluate the model performance later. Data split appears to be one of the major causes of leaking data to both validation and test sets [25] and hence needs to

---

[1] https://figshare.com/s/48cede3fffc2ff3c92df.

be done carefully. Leakage of data can be avoided by creating a proper split, late split, or applying data pre-processing steps before splitting the data into the train-test set. An empirical study [15] conducted on data leakage due to improper split in the context of AIOPs (AI for IT operations) found a noticeable impact of choosing proper split rather than random split which may reduce data leakage risk significantly. The case study considered random splitting, time-based splitting, and baseline splitting strategies while the train/validation ratio varied from 50%/50% to 90%/10%. The statistical test result showed the performance metrics were found significantly (Wilcoxon test; p-value¡0.05) higher for random splitting than the other two strategies and the authors concluded this as a consequence of data leakage occurred due to random split. For example, the average AUC for a random split in the 70%/30% ratio applied on Google and Backblaze datasets were 0.98 and 0.99 respectively while the values were 0.94 and 0.91 for the time-based split strategy. Nonetheless, the true positive and false positive rate was also found higher when random splitting was applied (0.98% and 0.99%) even though the dataset was imbalanced while for time-based splitting, these values were 0.64% and 0.7%. Based on the findings, the authors concluded the time-based split was found more appropriate for AIOPs model evaluation and less risk of data leakage. However, the authors did not apply other ways of splitting like cluster-based split and the dataset was for prediction task, not classification. In addition, time-based split could be appropriate for AIOPs data and for regression tasks nevertheless we employed image data for object detection tasks particularly in the context of automotive perception system.

Another study on exploring multiple data splitting strategies in the context of evaluating recommendation systems [17] concluded that the performance can be highly varied due to choosing improper data split but given with the same dataset and model. This work is also like prediction but not classification, where four different splitting strategies based on users and transactions were looked upon. These splitting strategies were applied on two different datasets and evaluated on multiple recommender models. The authors suggested temporal global splitting as the most realistic setting and it should be considered as default splitting strategy. They found temporal global splitting method achieved a recall of 0.3665 on the Tafeng dataset by the NGCF model and 0.1454 for the Dunnhumby dataset by the Triple2Vec model.

Doan et al. [5] introduced a new clustering-based within-class stratified splitting (WICS) technique to deal with small and imbalanced dataset problems in classification. Four classifiers were tested with varying hyper-parameters on a missile impact damage (MID) dataset and the models were evaluated in terms of recall, f1 score, kohen's kappa score and AUC. The results of WICS combined with SMOTE-NC sampling technique were highest for the support vector machine (SVM) classifier with f1-score 0.821, AUC value 0.949 with highly stable performance. However, the MID dataset is a small dataset and each data point belongs to one single class which is unlike to more complex scenarios like in traffic where multi-class road users are present in a single frame. [2] also brought up the complexity that occurs with the presence of multiple-type instances in a single image where the classifier has to correctly identify regions and which class it may belong based on the highest confidence value of the model. Hence, the application of sampling techniques like SMOTE-NC or stratified sampling on this type of mixed data will not help to eradicate class imbalance.

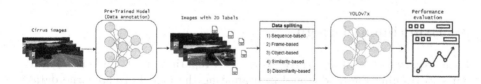

Fig. 1. The Graphical Overview of the experiment.

Wenyan Wu and her colleagues introduced a method [27] to compare different data splitting methods and proved that the data splitting techniques have a significant impact on the performance of ANN models. This happens due to potential bias and variance of the models introduced by the chosen data split and the process of model generation. They tested three data splitting methods on two different rainfall-runoff forecasting datasets and concluded that different data splitting methods exhibit different biases to the model performance. Among the three splitting methods, DUPLEX was found to result in comparatively low bias and variance but at the same time, it is slightly pessimistic in terms of performance estimation. The mean RMSE values reported from the DUPLEX splitting method is 3889 for the Kentucky dataset and 6.53 for the Necker dataset while for both datasets, bias was 10.61% and 25.57% respectively. The suggested DUPLEX method draws samples based on Euclidean distances, the farthest two points are assigned to one set, and the next two farthest points are assigned to another set and so on. It is an old method developed by Snee [21] in 1977 for validating regression models but usability for complex classification tasks like object detection in traffic scenarios is not justified yet.

The popular benchmark datasets for autonomous driving such as Kitti [6] and nuScenes [3] often come with predefined splits into train and evaluation sets to ease bench-marking various object detection models. However, how the split was done and based on which strategy are not always clearly explained. The mentioned datasets are some of the well-known and popular in the AD field but also relatively old (2013 and 2019). This work brought a newly introduced dataset called Cirrus [24] in use which was introduced in 2021 and has a higher image resolution of 1920 X 650. The dataset also got attention due to its unique sequences with roughly 891 frames per sequence, collected from different real driving scenarios on highways and urban roads. This research aimed to look into the impact of several data splitting techniques applied on the cirrus dataset from a different point of view such as separating data based on sequences and also mixing them before splitting to see how the performance differs when split is done based on time, object, similarity and dissimilarity criteria. The YOLOv7 model is one of the latest editions in the YOLO (You Only Look Once) family, which is very popular [10] for being a lighter and faster object detection model. YOLOv7x employed a trainable bag-of-freebies method that enhances the accuracy of 2D-object detection. According to a recent survey [4] on object detection, YOLOv7 is the state-of-the-art method that surpasses existing object detection methods in terms of accuracy and speed without increasing the inference cost [23].

3 Experiment Design

Each experiment contains three steps: 1) Preparing the train-validation-test data, 2) training the model, and 3) evaluating the model. To split the dataset into train, validation, and test sets, six splitting strategies were applied. After that, the YOLOv7x object detection model [23], which is a variation of YOLOv7 has been employed on each split. The trained model was evaluated later with the validation dataset. Figure 1 shows the overview of the experimental setup and the steps.

3.1   Data Preparation

Cirrus [24] is an open-source dataset for autonomous driving from Volvo cars. It contains 6285 RGB images along with their corresponding 3D point clouds. However due to a lack of proper calibration matrices and the absence of enough supporting information on how to translate the annotations, mapping of the 3D points was not possible and thus 3D annotations coming with the images could not be utilized for this experiment. So, we generated the 2D labels for all cirrus RGB images using the inference of YOLOv7. Wang's YOLOv7 object detection models had been pre-trained using the MS COCO dataset which contains 80 different classes, but only eight of them were present in Cirrus. These are Person, Bicycle, Car, Motorcycle, Bus, Truck, Traffic Light, and Stop Sign. After the 2D labeling with inference, images were manually checked to see whether the labels

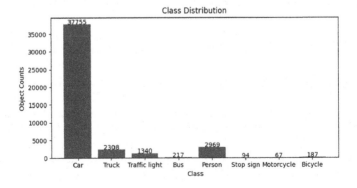

Fig. 2. The Cirrus class distributions with 8 classes.

were correct and bounding boxes surrounding the objects were drawn perfectly. The class distribution of these 8 class labels present in all the 6285 images of the Cirrus dataset is shown in Fig. 2. Once the labels are created for all Cirrus images, different splitting techniques can be applied as individual treatments. A conclusion could be drawn later on once the performance of each of the trained models with different splits is compared with the hypothesis using statistical analysis methods.

3.2   Treatments – Independent Variable

The Cirrus dataset consists of seven individual folders in total which contain consecutive frames of seven different video segments (see Fig. 3) and each of the folders is called an individual sequence later in this paper. To investigate different splitting techniques, all seven sequences of image frames were used with different combinations in every treatment. As a standard practice, the train-validation-test split was always applied throughout the treatments although the validation set is usually used for hyper-parameter tuning and model optimization to ensure better performance on the test data. The name and the splitting technique of each of the treatments are described below:

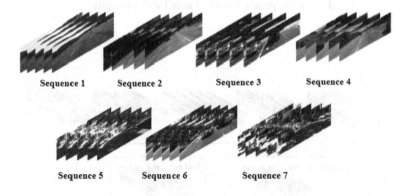

Fig. 3. Image Sequences of Cirrus Dataset.

3.2.1   Treatment 1: Sequence-Based Split (ThreeTwoTwo). The first treatment is generated using all seven Cirrus image sequences and using combinations of sequences as input: 3 sequences in the train set, 2 sequences in the validation set, and 2 sequences in the test set (as like Fig. 4). This was done by randomly choosing the different combinations of sequences to put them in three different sets naming train, validation, and test set. The idea behind choosing this particular combination is to make the data proportion balanced by putting comparatively more data into the train set than the validation and test sets. The treatment was repeated 10 times in the form of trials with different train-validation-test data every time to neutralize randomness.

3.2.2 Treatment 2: Sequence-Based Split (FiveOneOne).

The second treatment is another form of sequence-based treatment where 5 sequences belong to the train set, 1 sequence each to the validation and test set (as in Fig. 5). This combination is chosen to increase the train set volume than in treatment 1 but keep the validation and test sets equal in size. Sequence selection in this treatment is also done by randomly choosing the different combinations every time repeated as 10 individual trials.

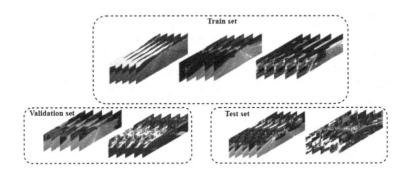

Fig. 4. Sequence-based (ThreeTwoTwo) split.

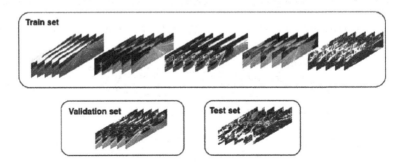

Fig. 5. Sequence-based (FiveOneOne) split.

3.2.3 Treatment 3: Frame-Based Split (4 Frames - 1 Frame).

This treatment contains a form of frame-based split where not each of the image sequences was considered individually but all the image sequences together where consecutive 4 image frames went to the train set and every 5th frame went to the validation/test set and so on (see Fig. 6). As the image frames come from video segments, the difference between consecutive frames can be small. In this way, the train set images have more similarity to the validation/test set images.

3.2.4   Treatment 4: Object-Based Split. To prepare this treatment, all the images are combined together and then the images containing a single type of object (e.g., Cars) are separated and put into the train set and the rest of the data are put into the validation set (Fig. 7). The idea behind this type of split is to examine the model to detect known objects in a mixed environment where other types of objects are also present.

3.2.5   Treatment 5: Similarity-Based Split. The similarity-based split is one of the most interesting splitting techniques, especially for this piece of work. In order to do the similarity-based split, the pair-wise similarity at the pixel level of all the image pairs was calculated as the first step. There are several metrics available like Root Mean Square Error (RMSE), Structural Similarity Index (SSiM), etc. to calculate pixel-level similarities between images. Initially, both RMSE and SSiM were considered as both are popular and frequently used but in this experiment, the RMSE was chosen because we found that the calculation time for RMSE was significantly shorter than the SSiM for the Cirrus data. As the data contains over 6,000 images, which leads to approximately 2 million image pair combinations to be calculated, even a small calculation time difference for each image pair can have a significant performance impact.

Hierarchical clustering was then applied to merge the images until three groups/clusters were formed to be used as train, validation, and test sets. As RMSE is basically the distance between images, the lower value means the higher

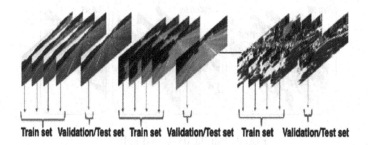

Train set Validation/Test set Train set Validation/Test set Train set Validation/Test set

Fig. 6. Frame-based Splits.

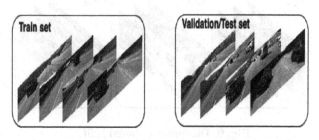

Fig. 7. Object-based split

similarity and hence the groups were formed based on the lowest values of RMSE between image pairs. An example of this split is illustrated in Fig. 8.

3.2.6   Treatment 6: Dissimilarity-Based Split. This treatment is the variation of the previous treatment 5 where we considered the same RMSE values but in descending order. That means the hierarchical clustering was applied to form three clusters based on the highest RMSE values (the most distinct images). See the example illustrated in Fig. 9.

3.3   Pipeline

The ML pipeline used in this work is the pre-trained YOLOv7x model which was pre-trained on the MS COCO dataset. YOLOv7x is basically a variation of the YOLOv7 object detection model with better accuracy than the base model according to the chart mentioned in [23]. The model is provided the image data along with the object labels in a specific format to the train, validation, and test data folders. For each of the experiments, this train, validation and test data folders were populated by the data from the desired treatments (splits) before training the YOLOv7x base model every time. To evaluate the trained models, the designated scripts need to be executed by providing necessary hyperparameters such as epochs and batch size accordingly.

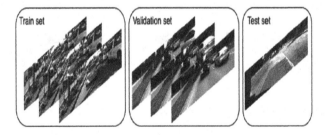

Fig. 8. Similarity-based split.

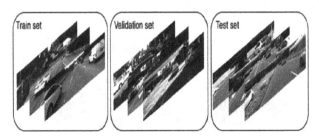

Fig. 9. Dissimilarity-based split.

3.4   Tasks

The basic task of this work is to perform object detection in 2D images using the YOLOv7 [23] network. But the ultimate bigger goal is to investigate different data splits when they are applied (i.e., train-validation-test data portion varies), and how the models' performance gets affected. The images are coming from the Cirrus dataset as mentioned in previous sections. There are eight categories or classes in total in the Cirrus images. The classes are Person, Bicycle, Car, Motorcycle, Bus, Truck, Traffic Light and Stop Sign. YOLOv7x, a modification of the YOLOv7 object detection model is used to perform the designated task. The model will be trained and evaluated for each treatment with varied data in training and validation/test sets according to the splits.

3.5   Dependent Variable

The dependent variable is the mean average precision (mAP) used to compare the performance of each data split-based trained model. The mean average precision (mAP) is widely adopted by the computer vision research community [9,12,13] as a standard metric to assess the stability of object detection models [14]. The mean average precision (mAP) for object detection is the mean of APs (Average Precision) calculated for all the classes. The mAP encompasses the balance between precision and recall and optimizes the impact of both measures. However, this study did not consider measures like FPs and FNs separately because they are already considered during precision and recall calculation. Nonetheless, the main focus of this study is to investigate performance differences for different data splits applied prior to training and model evaluation so adding more measures will add extra complexity during comparison. The formula of mAP calculation is presented in Eq. 1:

$$mAP = \frac{1}{n} \sum_{k=1}^{k=n} AP_k \qquad (1)$$

Where, AP_k = Average Precision (AP) of class k, n = The number of classes.

This experiment considered mAP for comparison which is automatically calculated and generated by the yolov7x model at the end of each trial so no manual calculation is required It helps to avoid possibilities of minor rounding and truncation errors and thus makes mAP the fairest measure to be nominated as the dependent variable for comparison.

3.6   Hypotheses

The null hypothesis of this investigation study is that the means of the mean average precision (mAP) for each of the treatments with different splits will be equal or indifferent for all validation and test datasets. So the hypothesis for validation sets is:

$$\mu_{mAPt1_{\text{val}}} = \mu_{mAPt2_{\text{val}}} = \mu_{mAPt3_{\text{val}}} = \mu_{mAPt4_{\text{val}}} =$$
$$\mu_{mAPt5_{\text{val}}} = \mu_{mAPt6_{\text{val}}} \quad (2)$$

And the hypothesis for test sets is:

$$\mu_{mAPt1_{\text{test}}} = \mu_{mAPt2_{\text{test}}} = \mu_{mAPt3_{\text{test}}} = \mu_{mAPt4_{\text{test}}} =$$
$$\mu_{mAPt5_{\text{test}}} = \mu_{mAPt6_{\text{test}}} \quad (3)$$

3.7   Analysis Methods

To analyze the findings for each of the treatments or in other words to verify whether the null hypothesis can be rejected or not, the Kruskal-Wallis test [16], a non-parametric statistical test would be applied. As there is one dependent variable from six treatments in this experiment and normal distribution of the values can't be guaranteed, the Kruskal-Wallis test seems the best fit to analyze the variance of the dependent variable (mAP in this case).

3.8   Experimental Setup

We used the default hyper-parameters of YOLOv7x[2] during our experiments because our study does not focus on increasing the performance of object detection but instead investigates the impact of different data splitting strategies on the ML model performance. Also, using different hyper-parameter values for different treatments will introduce explicit bias to the model which might infect the result of our comparative analysis of different splitting techniques. We run our experiments for up to 100 epochs with a batch size of 16. Moreover, the YOLOv7x model was examined with one data split method for 50, 200, and 500 epochs. Our analysis indicates that the training converges with 100 epochs, becomes under-fitted with 50 epochs, and over-fitted with 500 epochs.

All the experiments were conducted on a server with an Intel Core-i7 CPU @ 3.70 GHz, 32.0 GB of RAM, and an additional NVIDIA GeForce RTX 4090 GPU. By testing repeatedly, it was observed that the server might only complete running one experiment with a batch size of 16.

4   Evaluation Results

To compare the results of each of the treatments, the dependent variable mean average precision (mAP) was considered.

---

[2] https://github.com/WongKinYiu/yolov7

4.1   Treatment 1: Sequence-Based Split (ThreeTwoTwo)

The experiment with this split was conducted 10 times with different combinations of sequences put into each of the train, validation, and test sets every time. The combination of the image sequences was selected completely randomly which of them will be in the train set and which of them will be in the validation and test set. Each image sequence has been given a serial ID to uniquely denote them and for better understanding with transparency, all the selected combinations are given in Table 1 along with the image sequence IDs.

As the combinations of all image sequences in the train, validation, and test set are varied, the class-specific mAP also varied for each of the trials. The graph in Figs. 10a and 10b shows how the mAP varied for all classes in each of the 10 trials for both validation and test datasets. It must also be mentioned that the mAP score varied most and/or low mAP for the classes with less frequency in the distribution graph (Fig. 2).

4.2   Treatment 2: Sequence-Based Split (FiveOneOne)

This treatment is another sequence-based treatment used in this work which also combines several image sequences for the train set and a single image sequence for both the validation and test set. As like the other sequence-based ThreeTwoTwo split, this treatment was also repeated 10 times with different combinations of sequences chosen completely randomly to avoid biasness. The combinations of image sequences are given in Table 1 for transparency.

Table 1. Sequences used in each trials for treatment 1 & 2.

Treatment No.	Trial No.	Train set	Validation set	Test set
Treat. 1	1	1, 4, 7	2, 5	3, 6
	2	1, 2, 3	4, 5	6, 7
	3	2, 3, 4	5, 6	7, 1
	4	3, 4, 5	6, 7	1, 2
	5	4, 5, 6	7, 1	2, 3
	6	5, 6, 7	1, 2	3, 4
	7	6, 7, 1	2, 3	4, 5
	8	7, 1, 2	3, 4	5, 6
	9	1, 3, 7	2, 6	4, 5
	10	2, 4, 6	1, 3	5, 7
Treat. 2	1	1, 2, 3, 4, 5	6	7
	2	2, 3, 4, 5, 6	7	1
	3	3, 4, 5, 6, 7	1	2
	4	4, 5, 6, 7, 1	2	3
	5	5, 6, 7, 1, 2	3	4
	6	6, 7, 1, 2, 3	4	5
	7	7, 1, 2, 3, 4	5	6
	8	1, 3, 5, 6, 7	2	4
	9	1, 2, 4, 6, 7	3	5
	10	2, 3, 4, 5, 7	1	6

Similar to the previous sequence-based ThreeTwoTwo split, the bar graph of the mAP scores for each of the classes of this treatment are also unevenly distributed (see Figs. 10c and 10d). That means when the image sequences are mixed up randomly for every trial, the number of object classes present in the training set varied and hence the performance on validation and test data also varied. It is also noticeable in the graphs that the mAP score for the 'Stop Sign' class is the lowest and often absent for some of the trials. It happened because of the lower number of occurrences of this class label in the whole dataset.

4.3 Treatment 3: Frame-Based Split

The frame-based split contains four consecutive frames in the train set and all fifth frames are separated into a validation/test set. For the sake of running balanced experiments, the validation/test set was further split into two sets by putting 50% in each set to be treated as validation and test sets. The mAP scores for both the validation and test set are summarized in Table 2.

Table 2. Summary of average mAP values for all 6 splits

Data splits	mAP validation	mAP test
ThreeTwoTwo	0.594	0.488
FiveOneOne	0.605	0.502
Frame-based	0.894	0.633
Object-based	0.118	0.110
Similarity-based	0.943	1.0
Dissimilarity-based	0.821	0.754

4.4 Treatment 4: Object-Based Split

In this treatment, all the images containing only the 'Car' object are put into the train set, and the rest are put in the validation/test set. Similar to treatment 3, this mixed set was further divided into two sets to feed as validation and test set to the model. 50% images were chosen randomly to form these two sets. The mAP scores on both validation and test sets are given in Table 2.

4.5 Treatment 5: Similarity-Based Split

The similarity-based split was applied by mixing all the image sequences and using the hierarchical clustering technique to cluster based on the pairwise similarity scores. Applying this, three clusters were formed which were used as train, validation, and test sets. As an unsupervised learning algorithm, the hierarchical clustering auto calculates and generates the results. The idea was to not interfere

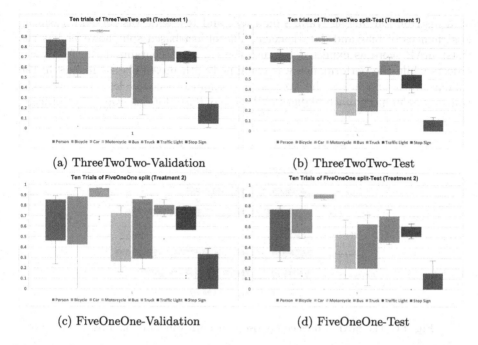

(a) ThreeTwoTwo-Validation   (b) ThreeTwoTwo-Test

(c) FiveOneOne-Validation   (d) FiveOneOne-Test

Fig. 10. The mAP for validation sets and test sets of each trial for both treatments 1 and 2.

with this process and keep it as genuine and realistic as possible so that more expansive results come out. The mAP scores for both validation and test sets are given in Table 2.

4.6   Treatment 6: Dissimilarity-Based Split

This treatment used the same techniques as treatment 5 but it considered the minimum similarity values to form the clusters so that the dissimilarity-based clusters are formed at the end. The three clusters generated are considered as the train, validation, and test sets and the Table 2 contains the mAP scores for both validation and test sets.

4.7   Performance Comparison of All Treatments

From the bar graph in Fig. 11 it can be seen that the mAP score on the validation set for similarity-based split is 0.943 which is the highest among all 6 different splits scores. Also, the mAP scores for both frame-based and dissimilarity-based splits are greater than 0.8 (0.897 and 0.841 respectively) which are higher compared to the other three splits. It is because of the presence of highly similar images in train and validation/test sets. On the other hand, both the sequence-based splits have similar mAP scores of 0.594 and 0.605 which proves that the data distribution among train, validation, and test sets was random, assuring less chances of bias and data leakage. The object-based split however has the worst mAP score as expected because the train set contains data of only car objects while the performance was examined with mixed classes images in the validation set and hence the average performance becomes less. However, the trained model has a much higher mAP score of 0.916 for detecting 'Car' objects.

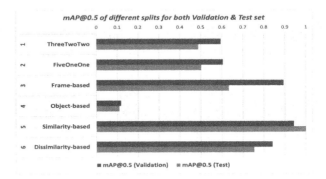

Fig. 11. The mAP scores comparison for both validation and test sets.

Figure 11 also shows the summary of the performance scores on the test sets for each of the treatments. The evaluation results on test sets followed the same pattern as the performance scores for validation sets except for the similarity-based split.

Table 3. Summary of the statistical tests.

Hypotheses	P-Values
Hypothesis 1 (mAP-valid)	5.583e-11 < 0.01
Hypothesis 2 (mAP-test)	8.452e-11 < 0.01

The Kolmogorov-Smirnov test [1] and the Shapiro-Wilk test [8] show that the data is not coming from normal distribution hence, a non-parametric test is required for the hypotheses test and would give more acceptable and realistic result. The Kruskal-Wallis test which is a non-parametric test and equivalent to the oneway-ANOVA parametric test, was performed on both the mAP values of the validation and test set for all different splits with a confidence level of 99%. The output of the test for both validation and test results showed that the null hypothesis can be rejected with a p-value <0.01 for both cases (see Table 3). Therefore, the mAP for both validation and test datasets are not the same for all six splits or there is a significant difference in model performance based on different data splits applied.

This means that the splitting technique applied when training and testing has a significant impact on the performance of the model. Now, we can dive deeper into the relationship between the splits, data leak probability, and model performance.

5 Discussion

In this study, we observed varying model performances across different data splits. Notably, the model exhibited the highest performance when images were grouped based on similarity, which serves as a robust baseline. Choosing a split with a high probability of similarity, while yielding optimal model performance, also raises concerns. This type of split, while boosting model accuracy, may lead to overly optimistic assessments and, in practical applications like autonomous driving, could result in safety hazards due to potential object detection failures.

A noteworthy observation is the high performance of the dissimilarity-based split. Its reliance on pixel-level similarity calculations introduces a measurement bias. For large images like those in the Cirrus dataset with 1920X1080 pixel resolution, the Root Mean Squared Error (RMSE) tends to converge toward the mean, limiting the practical utility of this split (using RMSE as a similarity measure) in certain contexts.

The frame-based split, which exposes every 5th image to the validation and test sets, showed the second-best performance. However, as this split neglects image properties, such as content, it is advisable to avoid it in real-world scenarios to prevent unintended biases. The object-based split, utilizing semantic information about objects, intentionally biases the split by training on only one class (Cars). It highlights the significance of ensuring a comprehensive representation of all classes for optimal model performance. The intentional bias underscores the importance of exposing models to a diverse range of objects and traffic situations to enhance their generalization capabilities.

The FiveOneOne and ThreeTwoTwo scenarios, representing training in one geographical location and testing/validating in others, emerged as the most realistic. Hence, these scenarios provide a representative sample of real-world conditions. Although their performance is lower (0.594 and 0.605), they ensure a more accurate reflection of model capabilities emphasizing the importance of a careful data split.

The results were presented to our industrial partner and they decided to change their data split from a frame-based split (Treatment 3) to a variation of Treatment 1 (and Treatment 2) including more meta-data for their perception pipeline. Although our results are different across different splitting methods for the Cirrus dataset, further investigation is needed to generalize these findings for other datasets where image samples are independent.

6 Threats to Validity

We use the framework provided by Wohlin et al. [26] to discuss the four categories of threats to validity: conclusion, internal, construct, and external.

Conclusion Validity: Concerns regarding the conclusion validity revolve around factors that can impact the capacity to arrive at an accurate judgment regarding the connections between the treatment and the results of an experiment.

Reliability of measure. The mAP measure used as the dependent variable in this experiment may not necessarily be always reliable. Changes in class occurrences in different treatments might result in different APs of individual classes which can have an impact on the mAP scores. This threat is planned to be overcome in the future by ensuring a more balanced class distribution for individual splits.

Reliability of treatment implementation. As the splits are not always controlled by any parameter like class/instance counts, the class distribution might be different for each of the splits which may affect performance. This threat was not possible to mitigate in this experiment and will be considered during the future experiments design.

Internal Validity: Threats to internal validity encompass factors that may impact the independent variable's causality without the researcher's awareness, thereby jeopardizing the ability to draw a definitive conclusion regarding a potential cause-and-effect relationship between the treatment and the outcome.

Maturation. The object detection model was trained for 100 epochs for all six treatments regardless of considering any threshold of loss or accuracy. This might introduce a maturation threat due to differences in data points for the treatments. To mitigate this, the model was trained for 500 epochs for the majority of treatments and the increase found was not significant in performance measure (between 0.006 and 0.009).

Instrumentation. The 2D labels used in this experiment were generated with the inference of a pre-trained model so there is a risk of instrumentation threat. It was mitigated by manually checking the drawn bounding boxes on all images and removing erroneous items.

Construct Validity: Construct validity pertains to the extent to which the findings of an experiment can be applied or extended to the underlying concept or theory that forms the basis of the experiment.

Mono-operation bias. The experiment focused only on the object detection task and used the related dataset and performance measure to find the impact of different data splits which may contain mono-operation bias threats. Some other operations like image segmentation are also planned to be performed in future experiments focusing on the impact of data leaks through different splits.

Mono-method bias. The mAP is calculated using the confusion matrix, intersection over union (IoU), precision and recall but it does not give equal weight to both precision and recall which may invoke a mono-method bias threat. However other measures like the f1-score could also be considered where both precision and recall get the same importance. Although there is always a trade-off between precision and recall, future experiments related to data splits and finding data leaks will consider both mAP and f1-score to establish firm hypotheses.

Confounding constructs and levels of constructs. Different treatments considered different ways of splitting the data and it results differences in the number of images in train and validation/test sets particularly for similarity/dissimilarity-based splits as the splitting techniques were not controlled due to the use of unsupervised clustering methods.

External Validity: Factors affecting external validity are circumstances that restrict our capacity to apply the outcomes of our experiment to real-world industrial scenarios.

Interaction of setting and treatment. One external threat could be the use of the yolov7x object detection model only. Other 2D object detection models might give different mAP values. However, the use of other models was not in the scope of the experiment and the literature mentioned earlier suggests that the YOLOv7x model qualifies as the best choice because of benefits like high performance and speed.

Interaction of selection and treatment. The class imbalance exists in the cirrus dataset can also be considered as an external threat to validity. Although having a perfectly balanced dataset for such image recognition and object detection task is difficult and most of the popular benchmark datasets are not balanced however, repeating the experiment with other datasets which are comparatively less imbalanced would help to generalize the findings of this experimental study.

Interaction of history and treatment. Another external validity threat comes from the selection of the data – one dataset from an automotive OEM. Using more datasets is the mainstream of our current work.

7   Conclusion and Future Work

This study explored various data splits to evaluate machine learning model performance in object detection tasks. Findings revealed that splits based on image similarity and frame sequences exhibited commendable performance. The FiveOneOne and ThreeTwoTwo split scenarios emerged as the safest choices from the discussion which are closely resembling real-world situations without compromising data integrity.

The study also emphasized the importance of choosing the right data split and the need for complete and diverse training sets to develop safe and effective vision systems. The object-based split was found to be effective in utilizing semantic information about objects. However, intentionally preparing a biased split that lacked all objects highlighted the risk of overly restricting model performance.

Interestingly, the dissimilarity-based split showed high performance. However, the study found a built-in measurement bias due to pixel-level similarity calculation, limiting its practical use. This study highlights appropriate data splits and diverse training data's crucial role in developing safe and effective machine learning models for automotive software.

In future work, we are planning to explore alternative ways of splitting data that can tackle data leaks and object-based class imbalance problems while maintaining high model performance. We are also planning to conduct similar experiments on different domain-specific images considering different semantic-level image similarity measures to make our study generalizable. Additionally, further investigation into the impact of diverse training sets on model performance and autonomous driving safety in real-world scenarios could be beneficial.

References

1. Berger, V.W., Zhou, Y.: Kolmogorov-smirnov test: overview. Wiley StatsRef: Statistics reference online (2014)
2. Boukerche, A., Hou, Z.: Object detection using deep learning methods in traffic scenarios. ACM Comput. Surv. (CSUR) **54**(2), 1–35 (2021)
3. Caesar, H., et al.: nuScenes: a multimodal dataset for autonomous driving. In: Proceedings of the IEEE/CVF Conference on Computer Vision and Pattern Recognition, pp. 11621–11631 (2020)
4. Cheng, G., et al.: Towards large-scale small object detection: survey and benchmarks. IEEE Trans. Pattern Anal. Mach. Intell. (2023)
5. Doan, Q.H., Mai, S.H., Do, Q.T., Thai, D.K.: A cluster-based data splitting method for small sample and class imbalance problems in impact damage classification. Appl. Soft Comput. **120**, 108628 (2022)
6. Geiger, A., Lenz, P., Stiller, C., Urtasun, R.: Vision meets robotics: the kitti dataset. Int. J. Robot. Res. **32**(11), 1231–1237 (2013)
7. Gupta, A., Anpalagan, A., Guan, L., Khwaja, A.S.: Deep learning for object detection and scene perception in self-driving cars: survey, challenges, and open issues. Array **10**, 100057 (2021)
8. Hanusz, Z., Tarasinska, J., Zielinski, W.: Shapiro-Wilk test with known mean. REVSTAT-Stat. J. **14**(1), 89–100 (2016)
9. Huang, Z., Wang, J., Fu, X., Yu, T., Guo, Y., Wang, R.: DC-SPP-YOLO: dense connection and spatial pyramid pooling based yolo for object detection. Inf. Sci. **522**, 241–258 (2020)
10. Jiang, P., Ergu, D., Liu, F., Cai, Y., Ma, B.: A review of yolo algorithm developments. Procedia Comput. Sci. **199**, 1066–1073 (2022)
11. Kiran, B.R., et al.: Deep reinforcement learning for autonomous driving: a survey. IEEE Trans. Intell. Transp. Syst. **23**(6), 4909–4926 (2021)
12. Kosuge, A., Suehiro, S., Hamada, M., Kuroda, T.: mmWave-YOLO: a mmWave imaging radar-based real-time multiclass object recognition system for ADAS applications. IEEE Trans. Instrum. Meas. **71**, 1–10 (2022)
13. Li, Y., Li, S., Du, H., Chen, L., Zhang, D., Li, Y.: YOLO-ACN: focusing on small target and occluded object detection. IEEE Access **8**, 227288–227303 (2020)
14. Liu, L., et al.: Deep learning for generic object detection: a survey. Int. J. Comput. Vision **128**, 261–318 (2020)
15. Lyu, Y., Li, H., Sayagh, M., Jiang, Z.M., Hassan, A.E.: An empirical study of the impact of data splitting decisions on the performance of AIOPs solutions. ACM Trans. Softw. Eng. Methodol. (TOSEM) **30**(4), 1–38 (2021)
16. McKight, P.E., Najab, J.: Kruskal-Wallis test. In: The Corsini Encyclopedia of Psychology, p. 1 (2010)

17. Meng, Z., McCreadie, R., Macdonald, C., Ounis, I.: Exploring data splitting strategies for the evaluation of recommendation models. In: Proceedings of the 14th ACM Conference on Recommender Systems, pp. 681–686 (2020)

18. Rashed, H., et al.: Generalized object detection on fisheye cameras for autonomous driving: dataset, representations and baseline. In: Proceedings of the IEEE/CVF Winter Conference on Applications of Computer Vision, pp. 2272–2280 (2021)

19. Redmon, J., Divvala, S., Girshick, R., Farhadi, A.: You only look once: unified, real-time object detection. In: Proceedings of the IEEE Conference on Computer Vision and Pattern Recognition, pp. 779–788 (2016)

20. Roriz, R., Cabral, J., Gomes, T.: Automotive lidar technology: a survey. IEEE Trans. Intell. Transp. Syst. **23**(7), 6282–6297 (2021)

21. Snee, R.D.: Validation of regression models: methods and examples. Technometrics **19**(4), 415–428 (1977)

22. Tu, F., Zhu, J., Zheng, Q., Zhou, M.: Be careful of when: an empirical study on time-related misuse of issue tracking data. In: Proceedings of the 2018 26th ACM Joint Meeting on European Software Engineering Conference and Symposium on the Foundations of Software Engineering, pp. 307–318 (2018)

23. Wang, C.Y., Bochkovskiy, A., Liao, H.Y.M.: Yolov7: trainable bag-of-freebies sets new state-of-the-art for real-time object detectors. arXiv preprint arXiv:2207.02696 (2022)

24. Wang, Z., et al.: Cirrus: a long-range bi-pattern lidar dataset. In: 2021 IEEE International Conference on Robotics and Automation (ICRA), pp. 5744–5750. IEEE (2021)

25. Wen, J., et al.: Convolutional neural networks for classification of Alzheimer's disease: overview and reproducible evaluation. Med. Image Anal. **63**, 101694 (2020)

26. Wohlin, C., Runeson, P., Höst, M., Ohlsson, M.C., Regnell, B., Wesslén, A.: Experimentation in Software Engineering. Springer, Heidelberg (2012). https://doi.org/10.1007/978-3-642-29044-2

27. Wu, W., May, R., Dandy, G.C., Maier, H.R.: A method for comparing data splitting approaches for developing hydrological ANN models (2012)

ML-Enabled Systems Model Deployment and Monitoring: Status Quo and Problems

Eduardo Zimelewicz[1] , Marcos Kalinowski[1(✉)] , Daniel Mendez[2,9] ,
Görkem Giray[3] , Antonio Pedro Santos Alves[1] , Niklas Lavesson[2] ,
Kelly Azevedo[1] , Hugo Villamizar[1] , Tatiana Escovedo[1] , Helio Lopes[1] ,
Stefan Biffl[4] , Juergen Musil[4] , Michael Felderer[5,6] , Stefan Wagner[7] ,
Teresa Baldassarre[8] , and Tony Gorschek[2,9]

[1] Pontifical Catholic University of Rio de Janeiro (PUC-Rio), Rio de Janeiro, Brazil
`kalinowski@inf.puc-rio.br`
[2] Blekinge Institute of Technology (BTH), Karlskrona, Sweden
[3] Izmir, Turkey
[4] Vienna University of Technology (TU Wien), Vienna, Austria
[5] German Aerospace Center (DLR), Cologne, Germany
[6] University of Cologne, Cologne, Germany
[7] Technical University of Munich, Munich, Germany
[8] University of Bari, Bari, Italy
[9] fortiss GmbH, Munich, Germany

Abstract. [Context] Systems that incorporate Machine Learning (ML) models, often referred to as ML-enabled systems, have become commonplace. However, empirical evidence on how ML-enabled systems are engineered in practice is still limited; this is especially true for activities surrounding ML model dissemination. [Goal] We investigate contemporary industrial practices and problems related to ML model dissemination, focusing on the model deployment and the monitoring ML life cycle phases. [Method] We conducted an international survey to gather practitioner insights on how ML-enabled systems are engineered. We gathered a total of 188 complete responses from 25 countries. We analyze the status quo and problems reported for the model deployment and monitoring phases. We analyzed contemporary practices using bootstrapping with confidence intervals and conducted qualitative analyses on the reported problems applying open and axial coding procedures. [Results] Practitioners perceive the model deployment and monitoring phases as relevant and difficult. With respect to model deployment, models are typically deployed as separate services, with limited adoption of MLOps principles. Reported problems include difficulties in designing the architecture of the infrastructure for production deployment and legacy application integration. Concerning model monitoring, many models in production are not monitored. The main monitored aspects are inputs, outputs, and decisions. Reported problems involve the absence of monitoring practices, the need to create custom monitoring tools, and the selection of suitable metrics. [Conclusion] Our results help provide a better understanding of

P. Bludau et al. (Eds.): SWQD 2024, LNBIP 505, pp. 112–131, 2024.
https://doi.org/10.1007/978-3-031-56281-5_7

the adopted practices and problems in practice and support guiding ML deployment and monitoring research in a problem-driven manner.

Keywords: Machine Learning · Deployment · Monitoring

1   Introduction

In recent years, the advancements in Machine Learning (ML) and, altogether, Artificial Intelligence (AI), have helped the incoming of technological innovation and transformation across various industries. These ML-enabled systems have shown capabilities in automating complex tasks, making data-driven decisions, and enhancing overall efficiency. However, despite their immense potential, the implementation of ML-enabled systems requires practitioners to adapt processes to successfully develop, deploy, and monitor in production operation. In the same level, Software Engineering (SE) practices can help to speed up the development of such features. However, ML-enabled systems are inherently different by nature affecting rendering traditional SE practices insufficient to be directly applied, thus, revealing new challenges [1].

In regard to the current increase in ML system usage, this paper aims to identify potential industrial problems and the current status quo in terms of practices applied in the development of ML-enabled software systems. With the main goal of understanding the pain points and how those systems are made, we conducted a questionnaire-based online survey. Although many other concerns appeared in the responses, such as issues in Requirements Engineering and Data Quality, the work presented in this paper focuses on the model deployment and monitoring of ML-enabled systems. Our focus is on evaluating experienced challenges as well as approaches employed.

The main findings show that practitioners perceive the model deployment and monitoring phases as relevant, but also challenging. With respect to model deployment, we observed that models are mainly deployed as separate services and that embedding the model within the consuming application or platform-as-a-service solutions are less frequently explored. Most practitioners do not follow MLOps principles and do not have an automated pipeline to retrain and redeploy the models, where the reported deployment problems include difficulties in designing the architecture of the infrastructure for production, considering scalability and financial constraints, and legacy application integration. Concerning model monitoring, many of the models in production are not monitored at all, with the main aspects in scope of monitored are being outputs and decisions taken. Reported problems include not having model appropriate monitoring practices in place, the need for developing customized monitoring tools, and difficulties choosing the appropriate metrics.

G. Giray—Independent Researcher.

The remainder of this paper is organized as follows. Section 2 provides the background and related work. In Sect. 3, we describe the research method. Section 4 presents then the results which we discuss further in Sect. 5. In Sect. 6, we critically reflect upon the threats to validity and mitigation actions before concluding our paper with Sect. 7.

2   Background and Related Work

Machine Learning (ML) has witnessed various advancements in recent years, transforming various industries by enabling intelligent decision-making systems. Deploying ML models into real-world applications, however, presents complex challenges related to model performance, reliability, and maintenance. This section provides an overview of the research landscape concerning the deployment and monitoring of Machine Learning systems.

The use of Machine Learning in practical applications dates back to the year of 1952 when English Mathematician Arthur Samuel created the first Machine Learning program to play championship-level game of checkers [2]. However, it is in the past decade that ML deployments have gained widespread attention in practice due to the availability of large datasets, more powerful computing hardware, and improved algorithms. Despite the rapid growth in ML adoption, there still exists a significant gap between the development of ML models in testing environments and their successful deployment in real-world settings, as reported by Paleyes et al. [3], especially in the fields of integration, monitoring, and updating a model. Further discussions show that, within the model deployment phase (which includes the monitoring part), adapting existing techniques such as DevOps could be extremely helpful to make development and production environments even closer, where the term MLOps follows the same concept by bringing together data scientists and operations teams, with Meenu et al. [4] identifying the activities and placing stages, by conducting a systematic literature review (SLR) and grey literature review (GLR), in which organizations can improve their MLOps adoption.

To represent the main issues to transition models to production architectures, some challenges were also identified and categorized by Lewis et al. [5] in four spaces. First, utilizing software architecture practices that are proven effective to traditional applications, but do not take into account the data driven aspect of such projects, meaning that the design and development of ML models, will have to be approached with new frameworks, as the one presented by Meenu et al. [6] Second, creating patterns and tactics to achieve ML Quality Attributes (QAs), where existing metrics will need to be revisited and new ones will be created to better evaluate systems. Third, the monitorability as a driving quality attribute, by having the infrastructure behind the monitoring platform to be responsible for collecting specific information related to changes in the dataset, as well as the incorporated user feedback, to observe the impacts to deployed ML systems. Fourth, co-architecting and co-versioning, where the architecture of the ML system itself, alongside the architecture that supports its life cycle, will have to be developed in sync, like the MLOps pipeline and the system integration, and the existing dataset as well as the programming code.

Apart from the architecture challenges, previous research has explored different deployment models for ML systems, as the SLR, and a GLR, conducted by Meenu *et al.* [7] by providing an overview of the AI deployment's status quo and practices to further design a deployment framework for these systems. Today's approaches range from traditional batch processing [8] to real-time streaming deployments [9] and, most currently, an increase in use of the cloud service offerings such as FaaS (Function as a Service) [10], SaaS (Software as a Service) [11], PaaS (Platform as a Service) [12] and IaaS (Infrastructure as a Service) [13], representing the benefits of cloud adoption by the practitioners such as the relief from the burden of servers' management, faster time to go into production, cost optimization and performance increase. Alongside the deployment models, the existing software architectures approaches are also getting adapted to ML models such as containerization [14], microservices [15], and serverless computing [16] have gained prominence in ensuring model deployment flexibility and scalability.

Recent studies have focused on the monitoring and maintenance of ML models. Researchers have proposed techniques for detecting Machine Learning specific metrics such as model drift, handling concept drift, and ensuring that models remain accurate and reliable over time [17,18], which involves concepts such as statistical process control, anomaly detection, and continuous integration/continuous deployment (CI/CD) practices.

The presented literature demonstrates the diverse nature of ML deployment and monitoring challenges. While numerous strategies and techniques have been proposed, there remains a need for a holistic framework that addresses these challenges and their current approach to solve them. Building upon the insights gained from the review of existing literature and the applied survey, this paper presents an overview to address the challenges of ML model deployments and monitoring. In the subsequent sections, we delve into the details of our research survey.

3   Research Method

3.1   Goal and Research Questions

The main goal of the research study focused on surveying the current status quo and problems through the entire development lifecycle of a ML system, but for the context of the current paper, the analysis will be based on two of the most problematic concerns in maintaining the model: (i) making the model available as quickly as possible in production and (ii) managing the model and re-training it along its continuous deployment based on monitored aspects. From this goal, we inferred the following research questions:

- RQ1. What are contemporary practices for deploying ML models?
  Under this question, we aim at identifying the in-use practices and trends of the *deployment* stage and can refine it further into three more detailed questions:

- RQ1.1. What kind of approaches are used to deploy ML models?
- RQ1.2. Which tools are used for automating model retraining?
- RQ1.3. What are the MLOps practices and principles used?
- RQ2. What are the main problems faced during the deployment in the ML life cycle stage?
- RQ3. What are contemporary practices for monitoring ML models?
  Under this question, we aim at identifying the in-use practices and trends of the *monitoring* stage and can refine it into two more detailed questions:
  - RQ3.1. What percentage of the ML-enabled system projects that get deployed into production have their ML models actually being monitored?
  - RQ3.2. What aspects of the models are monitored?
- RQ4. What are the main problems faced during the monitoring in the ML life cycle stage?
- RQ5. What is the percentage of projects that effectively go into production?

3.2   Survey Design

We designed our survey based on best community practices of survey research [19], carefully conducting, in essence, the following steps:

- **Step 1. Initial Survey Design.** We conducted a literature review on ML deployment and monitoring and combined our findings with previous results on problems and the status quo to provide the theoretical foundations for questions and answer options. From there, we drafted the initial survey by involving Software Engineering and Machine Learning researchers of PUC-Rio (Brazil) with experience in R&D projects involving ML-enabled systems.
- **Step 2. Survey Design Review.** The survey was reviewed and adjusted based on online discussions and annotated feedback from Software Engineering and Machine Learning researchers of BTH (Sweden). Thereafter, the survey was also reviewed by the other co-authors.
- **Step 3. Pilot Face Validity Evaluation.** This evaluation involves a lightweight review by randomly chosen respondents. It was conducted with 18 Ph.D. students taking a Survey Research Methods course at UCLM (Spain) taught by the second author. They were asked to provide feedback on the clearness of the questions and to record their response time. This phase resulted in minor adjustments related to usability aspects and unclear wording. The answers were discarded before launching the survey.
- **Step 4. Pilot Content Validity Evaluation.** This evaluation involves subject experts from the target population. Therefore, we selected five experienced data scientists developing ML-enabled systems, asked them to answer the survey, and gathered their feedback. The participants had no difficulties answering the survey, and it took an average of 20 min. After this step, the survey was considered ready to be launched.

The final survey started with a consent form describing the purpose of the study and stating that it is conducted anonymously. The remainder was divided into 15 demographic questions (D1 to D15) followed by three specific parts with 17 substantive questions (Q1 to Q17): 7 on the ML life cycle and problems, 5 on requirements, and 5 on deployment and monitoring. This paper focuses on the ML life cycle problems related to model deployment and aspects of monitoring, and the specific questions regarding problems motives. The excerpts of the questions we deem relevant in context of the paper at hands are shown in Table 1. The survey was implemented using the Unipark Enterprise Feedback Suite.

3.3   Data Collection

Our target population concerns professionals involved in building ML-enabled systems, including different activities, such as management, design, and development. Therefore, it includes practitioners in positions such as project leaders, requirements engineers, data scientists, and developers. We used convenience sampling, sending the survey link to professionals active in our partner companies, and also distributed it openly on social media. We excluded participants that informed having no experience with ML-enabled system projects. Data collection was open from January 2022 to April 2022. In total, we received responses from 276 professionals, out of which 188 completed all four survey sections. The average time to complete the survey was 20 min. We conservatively considered only the 188 fully completed survey responses.

3.4   Data Analysis Procedures

For data analysis purposes, given that all questions were optional, the number of responses varies across the survey questions. Therefore, we explicitly indicate the number of responses when analyzing each question.

Research questions $RQ1.1$, $RQ3.1$, $RQ3.2$, and $RQ5$ concern a mix of closed questions and optional free fields, so we decided to use inferential statistics to analyze them. Our population has an unknown theoretical distribution (i.e., the distribution of ML-enabled system professionals is unknown). In such cases, resampling methods - like bootstrapping - have been reported to be more reliable and accurate than inference statistics from samples [19,20]. Hence, we use bootstrapping to calculate confidence intervals for our results, similar as done in [21]. In short, bootstrapping involves repeatedly taking samples with replacements and then calculating the statistics based on these samples. For each question, we take the sample of n responses for that question and bootstrap S resamples (with replacements) of the same size n. We assume n as the total valid answers of each question [22], and we set 1000 for S, which is a value that is reported to allow meaningful statistics [23].

For research questions $RQ1.2$, $RQ1.3$, $RQ2$, $RQ3.1$ and $RQ4$, which seek to identify the main problems faced by practitioners involved in engineering ML-enabled systems related to model deployment and monitoring, alongside questions regarding which current practices are being applied, what amount of models that are generally available for users and the current monitored aspects, had their

Table 1. Research questions and survey questions

RQ	Survey No	Description	Type
-	...	...	...
RQ5	D7	How many ML-enabled system projects have you participated in? Please, provide your best estimate	Open
RQ5	D8	Of all the ML-enabled system projects you have participated in, how many were actually deployed into a production environment (e.g., released to the final customer)? Please, provide your best estimate:	Open
-	...	...	...
RQ2	Q4	According to your personal experience, please outline the main problems or difficulties (up to three) faced during each of the seven ML life cycle stages	Open
RQ4	Q4	According to your personal experience, please outline the main problems or difficulties (up to three) faced during each of the seven ML life cycle stages	Open
-	...	...	...
RQ1.1	Q13	In the context of the ML-enabled system projects you participated in, which approach is typically used to deploy ML models?	Multiple Option and Free Field
RQ1.2	Q14	Do you/your organization follow the practice and principles of ML-Ops in ML-enabled system projects? For instance, do you have an automated pipeline to retrain and deploy your ML models?	Single Option and Free Field
RQ1.3	Q14	Do you/your organization follow the practice and principles of ML-Ops in ML-enabled system projects? For instance, do you have an automated pipeline to retrain and deploy your ML models?	Single Option and Free Field
RQ3.1	Q15	Based on your experience, what percentage of the ML-enabled system projects that get deployed into production have their ML models actually being monitored?	Open
RQ3.2	Q16	Which of the following ML model aspects are monitored for the deployed ML-enabled system projects you have worked on?	Multiple Option and Free Field
-	...	...	...

corresponding survey question designed to be open text. We conducted a qualitative analysis using open and axial coding procedures from grounded theory [24] to allow the problems to emerge from the open-text responses reflecting the experience of the practitioners. The qualitative coding procedures were conducted by one PhD student, reviewed by her advisor at PUC-Rio, and reviewed independently by three researchers from two additional sites (two from BTH Sweden and one independent researcher from Turkey). The questionnaire, the collected data, and the quantitative and qualitative data analysis artifacts, including Python scripts for the bootstrapping statistics and graphs and the peer-reviewed qualitative coding spreadsheets, are available in our open science repository[1].

4 Results

All of the data that follows the study come with the bootstrapped samples together with the 95% confidence interval. The N in each figure caption is the number of participants that answered this question. We report the proportion P of the participants that checked the corresponding answer and its 95% confidence interval in square brackets.

4.1 Study Population

Figure 1 summarizes demographic information on the survey participants' countries, roles, and experience with ML-enabled system projects in years. It is possible to observe that the participants came from different parts of the world, representing various roles and experiences. While the figure shows only the ten countries with the most responses, we had respondents from 25 countries. As expected, our convenience sampling strategy influenced the countries, with most responses being from diverse countries (Brazil, Turkey, Austria, Germany, Sweden, and Italy).

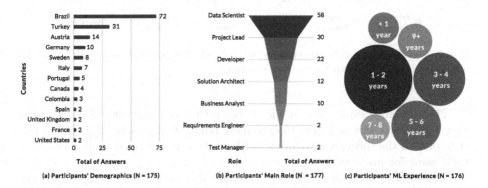

Fig. 1. Demographic graphs for participant's countries, roles and ML work experience

---

[1] https://doi.org/10.5281/zenodo.10092394.

Regarding employment, 45% of the participants are employed in large companies (2000+ employees), while 55% work in smaller ones of different sizes. It is possible to observe that they are mainly data scientists, followed by project leaders, developers, and solution architects. Regarding their experience with ML-enabled systems, most of the participants reported having 1 to 2 years of experience. Following closely, another substantial group of participants indicated a higher experience bracket of 3 to 6 years. This distribution highlights a balanced representation of novice and experienced practitioners. Regarding the participants' educational background, 81.38% mentioned having a bachelor's degree in computer science, electrical engineering, information systems, mathematics, or statistics. Moreover, 53.72% held master's degrees, and 22.87% completed Ph.D. programs.

4.2   Model Deployment and Monitoring Evaluation

In the survey, we used the same abstraction of seven generic life cycle phases of a popular Brazilian textbook on software engineering for data science [25]: problem understanding and requirements, data collection, data pre-processing, model creation and training, model evaluation, model deployment, and model monitoring. These phases were abstracted based on the nine ML life cycle phases presented by Amershi *et al.* [26] and the CRISP-DM industry-independent process model phases [27]. We asked about the perceived relevance and difficulty of each of the seven phases. For the purposes of this paper and for the sake of simplicity, we represent only the deployment and monitoring life cycle phases.

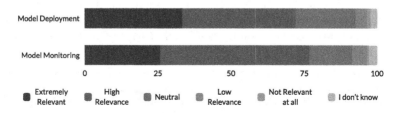

Fig. 2. Perceived relevance percentages of the Model Deployment and Model Monitoring activities according to survey participants

The relevance evaluation in Fig. 2 shows that the majority of respondents view these activities as highly to extremely relevant, it signifies the critical role they play in the software development life cycle, but still open to an increase in their value for projects.

Although respondents find those relevant, it does not necessarily reflect the expectations with the difficulty represented in Fig. 3, where the minority of practitioners find it complex up to very complex, possible due to the new solutions that come with a complete platform ready to have models deployed and, consequently, getting monitored out of the box.

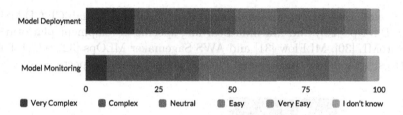

Fig. 3. Perceived difficulty percentages of Model Deployment and Model Monitoring activities according to survey participants

4.3 What Are Contemporary Practices for Deployment? (RQ1)

[RQ1.1] What Kind of Approaches Are Used to Deploy ML Models? For the first question of the survey regarding deployments, the participant were asked about which approach they usually take for hosting their models as shown in Fig. 4, where respondents could select more than one option. For the most part, *Service* was the top choice with $\mathbf{P = 59.457}$ **[59.219, 59.695]**, followed by *Embedded Models* with $\mathbf{P = 42.719}$ **[42.476, 42.962]** and *PaaS* with $\mathbf{P = 23.826}$ **[23.628, 24.024]**. Other solutions were also opened for answers and grouped in *Others* with $\mathbf{P = 5.47}$ **[5.359, 5.58]**.

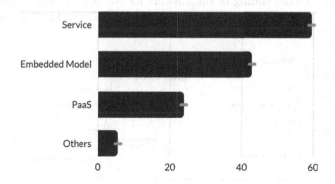

Fig. 4. Percentage of deployment approaches used by survey participants (N = 168)

[RQ1.2] Which Tools Are Used for Automating Model Retraining? and [RQ1.3] What Are the MLOps Practices and Principles Used? To describe the usage of MLOps in the life cycle, we asked if the respondents' organizations follow any of the practices or principles, followed by a follow up question if a foundational practice, such as an automated retraining pipeline, was used. The results are summarizsed in Fig. 5. The majority answered *No* with $\mathbf{P = 70.911}$ **[70.694, 71.128]** and, followed by *Yes* with $\mathbf{P = 29.089}$ **[28.872, 29.306]**. In regards to MLOps, some of the answers were between having their own pipeline built on top a continuous delivery tool (e.g. Gitlab CI/CD [28] and Azure DevOps [29]) and Machine Learning specific development platform such as BentoML [30], MLFlow [31] and AWS Sagemaker MLOps [32], which follows practices as model re-training and monitoring of relevant aspects.

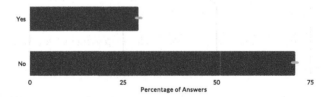

Fig. 5. Answers regarding the survey participant's organization usage of MLOps principles (N = 168)

4.4   What Are the Main Problems Faced During the Deployment in the ML Life Cycle Stage? (RQ2)

The survey had two questions regarding the main problems faced by practitioners through the deployment and monitoring of models. Figure 6 presents the results of the open and axial coding of the answers for the deployment phase using the probabilistic cause-effect diagrams introduced by Kalinowski *et al.* [33,34].

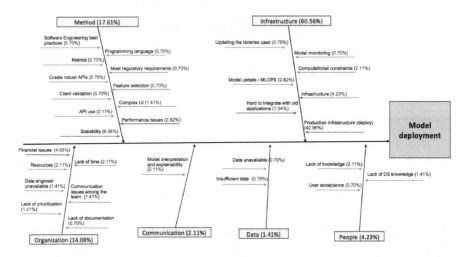

Fig. 6. Probabilistic cause-effect diagram related to answers regarding the main problems faced during the model deployment stage (N = 142)

As per the survey respondents, the top problems faced within the deployment phase were preparing the infrastructure for production deployment, the difficulty on integrating with legacy applications, what infrastructure architecture to use, how to scale it, and the financial limitations.

4.5   What Are Contemporary Practices for Monitoring? (RQ3)

[RQ3.1] What Percentage of the ML-Enabled System Projects that Get Deployed into Production Have Their ML Models Actually Being Monitored? To evaluate if the deployed projects went through the whole life cycle up until getting monitored, Fig. 7 shows that **P = 33.079 [32.842, 33.316]** participants responded that less than 20% of projects do get into production with their aspects monitored, followed by **P = 21.143 [20.942, 21.344]** responding from 20% to 40%, **P = 19.13 [18.943, 19.317]** answering that 80% to 100%, **P = 18.64 [18.456, 18.824]** from 40% to 60% and, finally, **P = 8.009 [7.874, 8.144]** with 60% to 80% get the released project monitored somehow.

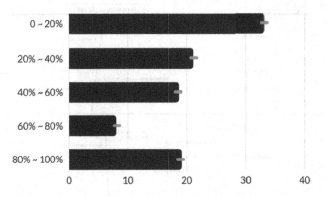

Fig. 7. Percentage of answers for models, deployed to production, that have their aspects monitored (N = 160)

[RQ3.2] What Aspects of the Models Are Monitored? Concerning the model monitoring, respondents described which monitoring aspects were actually monitored as in Fig. 8. Participants could be selecting more than one option, having *Input and Output* as the most frequent response with **P = 62.675 [62.431, 62.918]**, followed by *Output and Decisions* with **P = 62.082 [61.834, 62.331]**, *Interpretability Output* with **P = 28.034 [27.805, 28.263]**, *Fairness* with **P = 12.965 [12.792, 13.138]**, and other aspects that were grouped in *Others* with **P = 5.874 [5.761, 5.987]**.

4.6   What Are the Main Problems Faced During the Monitoring in the ML Life Cycle Stage? (RQ4)

Figure 9 presents the results of the open and axial coding of the answers for the main problems of the monitoring phase.

Fig. 8. Percentage of answers regarding which of the ML system aspects are monitored (N = 153)

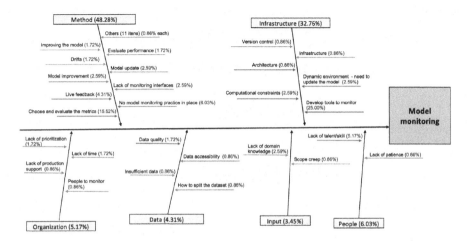

Fig. 9. Probabilistic cause-effect diagram related to answers regarding the main problems faced during the model monitoring stage (N = 116)

Here, the most observed concerns were related to the need of developing their own monitoring tools, evaluating and choosing the appropriate metrics, while not having any experience in monitoring models and in building monitoring platforms.

4.7   What Is the Percentage of Projects that Do Go into Production? (RQ5)

To describe the population of projects that live up until their general release, data from the demographic questions D7 and D8 (after data cleaning) were combined into Fig. 10. As this figure shows, **P = 24.965 [24.759, 25.171]** participants responded that between only 0% to 20% projects went into production, followed by **P = 23.553 [23.337, 23.768]** saying 40% to 60%, then **P = 21.221**

[21.029, 21.412] with 80% to 100%, **P = 17.796 [17.618, 17.974]** saying 20% to 40% and, finally **P = 12.465 [12.306, 12.624]** responding with 60% to 80%. By getting all of the percentages calculated and returning the mean value, this leaves us with an average of 45.41% of executed projects reaching general availability.

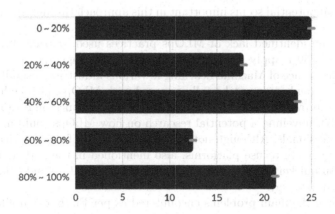

Fig. 10. The percentage of ML projects that do go into production (N = 169)

5 Discussion

Deploying Machine Learning models into production environments can be a complex and challenging task, often accompanied by several problems and considerations. As observed by the survey results as well, the model deployment and monitoring phases are found to be relevant by almost 75% of respondents, corroborating the importance of releasing it to the public and the constant performance analysis for a continuous increase on quality. Although to be found important, its difficulty rates decreased to almost 50% for deployment and 30% for monitoring, showing that a lack of opportunity to evaluate a model that is deployed into production could influence the entire development process analysis. For this case, Mäkinen *et al.* [35] surveyed data scientists to observe which type of organization would benefit from the MLOps practices, categorizing some of them as the top beneficiaries where the need for model retraining and deployment were extremely important to their natural next step into production models, showing a potential shift in the evaluation if more automated processes were applied to projects.

Through the deployment practices identified, it is evident that ML engineers are deploying most of their models through the Service approach, identifying a growing reliance on cloud-based services that offer comprehensive and scalable solutions already prepared, but compromising customization. Moreover, if integrating with external systems were found to be hard, Embedded Model seemed an alternative approach of choice, leveraging the operation efficiency of an existing software and faster response times, even though its monitoring and scaling difficulty were increased due to the lack of separation from the software that includes the model. At last, having the model deployed in a Platform as a Service approach promises to provide full customization of the infrastructure and flexible environment, although the increasing need for specialized expertise to enable its full potential seems important in this approach through such a complex system.

As per the identified lack of MLOps practices used, participants answered that less than 30% apply some of its principles. This suggests that despite the growing importance of Machine Learning in various industries, a significant number of professionals may not be fully engaged with MLOps, although numerous studies have proven its benefits [36] and providing guidance on establishing the platform [37], unveiling a potential research on how MLOps could influence the work of professionals. Although not fully applied, some of the practices do come embedded in ready to use platforms, also mentioned in the survey, facilitating the adoption quicker than by creating it from the ground up and expanding the usage in seamless way.

To enforce the main problems encountered as per Fig. 6, exemplified by this study as issues such as production level infrastructure management and integration with legacy systems, Nahar et al. [1] had a systematic literature review of challenges in building ML components. They revealed similar results related to deployment, the main challenges encountered along shifts from model-centric to pipeline-driven developments, difficulties in scaling model training and deployment on different types of hardware, and limited technical support for engineering infrastructure. For model monitoring, as per Fig. 9, it shows that choosing the metrics and developing new tools to adequate to project's monitoring necessities are the more prominent problems, where Nahar et al. observes that the monitorability of a model being considered late to be implemented, providing data quality due to not having well supported tools, lack of support to setup an infrastructure for detecting training-serving skew, and difficulty on designing specific metrics are aligned with the participants' feelings within the survey.

For the monitoring aspects, the survey highlights that the number of models that do go into production and have their aspects monitored are less than 50%, which highlights to us the potential on monitorability exploration for identifying aspects, detecting metrics, and creating new tools to increase the quality attributes of ML models. Following the current status of the monitoring phase, when participants have been asked which aspects were monitored, input and output data stands out. This emphasizes the critical role of data integrity and quality in the overall performance and robustness of Machine Learning systems by identifying potential biases, anomalies, and inconsistencies that could impact the accuracy and reliability of model predictions. Furthermore, monitoring the decisions assesses the correctness and effectiveness of model predictions and the process of decision making to validate the alignment between what was predicted and real-world outcomes. It also shows that the monitoring of interpretability output emerges as another prominent aspect, highlighting the increasing focus on enhancing the transparency and explainability of Machine Learning models, particularly crucial in domains such as establishing trust and verifying model behavior. Lastly, fairness monitoring demonstrates the growing recognition of the ethical implications of algorithms, spurring efforts to monitor and mitigate biases and discriminatory outcomes in model predictions, which underscores the commitment to developing inclusive and equitable Machine Learning systems.

As per Fig. 10, less than 50% of projects go into production, still showing a standing pattern where earlier reports [38, 39] and books [40] identified that most of the ML projects fail to get generally available due to several problems. Some of those were identified in this study and are possibly related, such as the organization being unable to fit the infrastructure to the needs of engineering teams, financial issues and not having sufficient expertise on the software engineering process that are, most likely, the lack of specialized professionals. As per Fig. 1, qualified personnel such as Cloud Infrastructure Engineers, Data Engineers, and Software Architects were not significantly identified in the team. However, due to the increasing value given to ML models deployment into production, articles such as Heymann *et al.* [41] will be in evidence to set a common place for frameworks, guides, and books responsible for developing production level ML models and how to apply them.

6 Threats to Validity

We identified some threats while planning, conducting, and analyzing the survey results. Hereafter, we list the most prominent threats organized by the survey validity types presented in [42].

Face and Content Validity. Face and content validity threats include bad instrumentation and inadequate explanation of the constructs. To mitigate these threats, we involved several researchers in reviewing and evaluating the questionnaire with respect to the format and formulation of the questions, piloting it with 18 Ph.D. students for face validity and with five experienced data scientists for content validity.

Criterion Validity. Threats to criterion validity include not surveying the target population. We clarified the target population in the consent form (before starting the survey). We also considered only complete answers (*i.e.*, answers of participants that answered all survey sections) and excluded participants that informed having no experience with ML-enabled system projects.

Construct Validity. We ground our survey's questions and answer options on theoretical background from previous studies [21, 43] and readings based on identified challenges in model deployment and monitoring [3] and in software architecture [5]. A threat to construct validity is inadequate measurement procedures and unreliable results. To mitigate this threat we follow recommended data collection and analysis procedures [19].

Reliability. One aspect of reliability is statistical generalizability. We could not construct a random sample systematically covering different types of professionals involved in developing ML-enabled systems, and there is yet no generalized knowledge about what such a population looks like. Furthermore, as a consequence of convenience sampling, the majority of answers came from Europe and South America, most of it from Brazil. Nevertheless, the experience and background profiles of the subjects are comparable to the profiles of ML teams as shown in Microsoft's study [44], showing that the nationality attribute did not interfered with the results. To deal with the random sampling limitation, we used bootstrapping and only employed confidence intervals, conservatively avoiding null hypothesis testing. Another reliability aspect concerns inter-observer reliability, which we improved by including independent peer review in all our qualitative analysis procedures and making all the data and analyses openly available online.

7   Conclusion

The current study sought to provide a comprehensive overview of the prevailing trends on practices and challenges in model deployment and monitoring within the context of Machine Learning. Through our questionnaire-based online survey targeting practitioners, we identified several key insights allowing us to elaborate as well on potential directions for future research and development. Our analysis underscores the increasing approach on leveraging cloud-based services for model deployment, with a notable emphasis on scalability, accessibility, and seamless integration. This should support the growing demand for efficient and user-friendly deployment solutions, catering to the diverse needs and constraints of contemporary applications. Furthermore, the emphasis on monitoring aspects reflects the heightened awareness of the critical role played by data quality, model accuracy, and transparency in ensuring the reliability and ethical soundness of Machine Learning models.

While the current work provides a comprehensive snapshot of the status quo, it also points towards several areas for further investigation and development. The increasing complexity of Machine Learning models and the dynamic nature of real-world applications, necessitate a more nuanced understanding of deployment and monitoring strategies that can adapt to diverse use cases and evolving challenges. Future research endeavors should prioritize the development of robust and scalable deployment frameworks that accommodate a wide range of ML models and their applications, focusing in better specific infrastructure management and seamless integration to other services. Additionally, there is a pressing need to advance methodologies for comprehensive and real-time monitoring, through incisive metrics discovery and ML-ready monitoring tools, enabling stakeholders to proactively identify and address potential biases, vulnerabilities, and performance bottlenecks in Machine Learning models.

The findings presented in this study contribute to the broader discourse surrounding the deployment and monitoring of Machine Learning models, highlighting the significance of holistic and adaptive approaches that prioritize reliability, interpretability, and observability. By leveraging the insights gleaned from this research, stakeholders and practitioners can take their efforts towards the responsible and impactful development of Machine Learning technologies and researchers can better root their ongoing research on practically relevant needs.

References

1. Nahar, N., Zhang, H., Lewis, G., Zhou, S., Kastner, C.: A meta-summary of challenges in building products with ml components - collecting experiences from 4758+ practitioners. In: 2023 IEEE/ACM 2nd International Conference on AI Engineering - Software Engineering for AI (CAIN), pp. 171–183. IEEE Computer Society, Los Alamitos, CA, USA, May 2023
2. Startech Up: Machine learning history: the complete timeline, September 2022
3. Paleyes, A., Urma, R.G., Lawrence, N.D.: Challenges in deploying machine learning: a survey of case studies. ACM Comput. Surv. **55**(6) (2022)
4. John, M.M., Olsson, H.H., Bosch, J.: Towards MLOps: a framework and maturity model. In: 2021 47th Euromicro Conference on Software Engineering and Advanced Applications (SEAA), pp. 1–8 (2021)
5. Lewis, G.A., Ozkaya, I., Xu, X.: Software architecture challenges for ml systems. In: 2021 IEEE International Conference on Software Maintenance and Evolution (ICSME), pp. 634–638 (2021)
6. John, M.M., Olsson, H.H., Bosch, J.: AI deployment architecture: multi-case study for key factor identification. In: 2020 27th Asia-Pacific Software Engineering Conference (APSEC), pp. 395–404 (2020)
7. John, M.M., Holmström Olsson, H., Bosch, J.: Architecting AI deployment: a systematic review of state-of-the-art and state-of-practice literature. In: Klotins, E., Wnuk, K. (eds.) ICSOB 2020. LNBIP, vol. 407, pp. 14–29. Springer, Cham (2021). https://doi.org/10.1007/978-3-030-67292-8_2
8. Zaharia, M., et al.: Apache spark: a unified engine for big data processing. Commun. ACM **59**(11), 56–65 (2016)
9. Syafrudin, M., Alfian, G., Fitriyani, N.L., Rhee, J.: Performance analysis of IoT-based sensor, big data processing, and machine learning model for real-time monitoring system in automotive manufacturing. Sensors **18**(9) (2018)
10. Chahal, D., Ojha, R., Ramesh, M., Singhal, R.: Migrating large deep learning models to serverless architecture, pp. 111–116 (2020). Cited by: 14
11. Nowrin, I., Khanam, F.: Importance of cloud deployment model and security issues of software as a service (SaaS) for cloud computing. In: 2019 International Conference on Applied Machine Learning (ICAML), pp. 183–186 (2019)
12. Mrozek, D., Koczur, A., Małysiak-Mrozek, B.: Fall detection in older adults with mobile IoT devices and machine learning in the cloud and on the edge. Inf. Sci. **537**, 132–147 (2020). Cited by: 72. All Open Access, Hybrid Gold Open Access (2020)
13. Abdelaziz, A., Elhoseny, M., Salama, A.S., Riad, A.: A machine learning model for improving healthcare services on cloud computing environment. Measurement **119**, 117–128 (2018)
14. Garg, S., Pundir, P., Rathee, G., Gupta, P., Garg, S., Ahlawat, S.: On continuous integration/continuous delivery for automated deployment of machine learning models using MLOps. In: 2021 IEEE Fourth International Conference on Artificial Intelligence and Knowledge Engineering (AIKE), pp. 25–28 (2021)

15. Al-Doghman, F., Moustafa, N., Khalil, I., Sohrabi, N., Tari, Z., Zomaya, A.Y.: AI-enabled secure microservices in edge computing: opportunities and challenges. IEEE Trans. Serv. Comput. **16**(2), 1485–1504 (2023)
16. Paraskevoulakou, E., Kyriazis, D.: ML-FaaS: towards exploiting the serverless paradigm to facilitate machine learning functions as a service. IEEE Trans. Netw. Serv. Manag. **20**, 2110–2123 (2023)
17. Kourouklidis, P., Kolovos, D., Noppen, J., Matragkas, N.: A model-driven engineering approach for monitoring machine learning models. In: 2021 ACM/IEEE International Conference on Model Driven Engineering Languages and Systems Companion (MODELS-C), pp. 160–164 (2021)
18. Schröder, T., Schulz, M.: Monitoring machine learning models: a categorization of challenges and methods. Data Sci. Manag. **5**(3), 105–116 (2022)
19. Wagner, S., Mendez, D., Felderer, M., Graziotin, D., Kalinowski, M.: Challenges in survey research. In: Contemporary Empirical Methods in Software Engineering, pp. 93–125. Springer, Cham (2020). https://doi.org/10.1007/978-3-030-32489-6_4
20. Lunneborg, C.E.: Bootstrap inference for local populations. Ther. Innov. Regul. Sci. **35**(4), 1327–1342 (2001)
21. Wagner, S., et al.: Status quo in requirements engineering: a theory and a global family of surveys. ACM Trans. Softw. Eng. Methodol. **28**(2) (2019)
22. Efron, B., Tibshirani, R.J.: An Introduction to the Bootstrap. Chapman & Hall/CRC (1993)
23. Lei, S., Smith, M.: Evaluation of several nonparametric bootstrap methods to estimate confidence intervals for software metrics. IEEE Trans. Software Eng. **29**(11), 996–1004 (2003)
24. Stol, K.J., Ralph, P., Fitzgerald, B.: Grounded theory in software engineering research: a critical review and guidelines. In: Proceedings of the 38th International Conference on Software Engineering, pp. 120–131 (2016)
25. Kalinowski, M., Escovedo, T., Villamizar, H., Lopes, H.: Engenharia de Software para Ciência de Dados: Um guia de boas práticas com ênfase na construção de sistemas de Machine Learning em Python. Casa do Código (2023)
26. Amershi, S., et al.: Software engineering for machine learning: a case study. In: 2019 IEEE/ACM 41st International Conference on Software Engineering: Software Engineering in Practice, pp. 291–300. IEEE (2019)
27. Schröer, C., Kruse, F., Gómez, J.M.: A systematic literature review on applying CRISP-DM process model. Procedia Comput. Sci. **181**, 526–534 (2021)
28. GitLab: Get started with GitLab CI/CD, October 2023
29. Azure DevOps: What is Azure DevOps? October 2022
30. BentoML: What is bentoml? October 2023
31. MLflow: What is mlflow? October 2023
32. AWS: Amazon SageMaker for MLOps, October 2023
33. Kalinowski, M., Mendes, E., Card, D.N., Travassos, G.H.: Applying DPPI: a defect causal analysis approach using Bayesian networks. In: Ali Babar, M., Vierimaa, M., Oivo, M. (eds.) PROFES 2010. LNCS, vol. 6156, pp. 92–106. Springer, Heidelberg (2010). https://doi.org/10.1007/978-3-642-13792-1_9
34. Kalinowski, M., Mendes, E., Travassos, G.H.: Automating and evaluating probabilistic cause-effect diagrams to improve defect causal analysis. In: Caivano, D., Oivo, M., Baldassarre, M.T., Visaggio, G. (eds.) PROFES 2011. LNCS, vol. 6759, pp. 232–246. Springer, Heidelberg (2011). https://doi.org/10.1007/978-3-642-21843-9_19

35. Mäkinen, S., Skogström, H., Laaksonen, E., Mikkonen, T.: Who needs MLOps: what data scientists seek to accomplish and how can MLOps help? In: 2021 IEEE/ACM 1st Workshop on AI Engineering - Software Engineering for AI (WAIN), pp. 109–112 (2021)
36. Ruf, P., Madan, M., Reich, C., Ould-Abdeslam, D.: Demystifying MLOps and presenting a recipe for the selection of open-source tools. Appl. Sci. **11**(19) (2021)
37. Zhou, Y., Yu, Y., Ding, B.: Towards MLOps: a case study of ML pipeline platform. In: 2020 International Conference on Artificial Intelligence and Computer Engineering (ICAICE), pp. 494–500 (2020)
38. Algorithmia: 2020 state of enterprise machine learning. Technical report (2019)
39. Siegel, E.: Models are rarely deployed: an industry-wide failure in machine learning leadership, January 2022
40. Weiner, J.: Why AI/Data Science Projects Fail: How to Avoid Project Pitfalls. Claypool Publishers, Morgan (2021)
41. Heymann, H., Kies, A.D., Frye, M., Schmitt, R.H., Boza, A.: Guideline for deployment of machine learning models for predictive quality in production. Procedia CIRP **107**, 815–820 (2022). Leading Manufacturing Systems Transformation - Proceedings of the 55th CIRP Conference on Manufacturing Systems (2022)
42. Linaker, J., Sulaman, S.M., Höst, M., de Mello, R.M.: Guidelines for conducting surveys in software engineering v. 1.1. Lund University 50 (2015)
43. Fernández, D.M., et al.: Naming the pain in requirements engineering: contemporary problems, causes, and effects in practice. Empir. Softw. Eng. **22**, 2298–2338 (2017)
44. Kim, M., Zimmermann, T., DeLine, R., Begel, A.: Data scientists in software teams: state of the art and challenges. IEEE Trans. Software Eng. **44**(11), 1024–1038 (2017)

Security and Compliance

Challenges of Assuring Compliance of Information Systems in Finance

Tomas Bueno Momčilović[✉][iD] and Dian Balta[iD]

fortiss GmbH, Munich, Germany
{momcilovic,balta}@fortiss.org
http://www.fortiss.org

Abstract. Assuring regulatory compliance of information systems (IS), as a bundle of software systems and business processes, is an important, but costly and continuous effort. Laws formulate demands for quality properties in ambiguous language, requiring substantial interpretation. Industry standards provide support, but remain generic and applicable to heterogeneous company IS contexts. Before compliance measures can be implemented in software assets and processes, a specific interpretation based on the context of each company is a prerequisite. Compliance experts such as auditors support this process by accounting for the perspectives of company stakeholders. Ultimately, however, the complexity of the required knowledge, legal and technical facets prevents organizations from continuously establishing situational awareness or guarantees, and answering the question: is the company currently compliant? We illustrate the complexity of assuring compliance in a qualitative case study with a European, software-driven corporation in the financial industry. Through modeling of an example of annual audits and analyzing literature, we describe the perspectives of the involved stakeholders with their roles, knowledge needs and facets. We observe six challenges: (1) large number of items and links; (2) unclear and implicit links; (3) siloing of knowledge; (4) multiple sources of truth; (5) high costs of learning from audits; and (6) uncertain results of traditional auditing. We discuss the implications of these observed challenges, and briefly explore potential avenues for resolution.

Keywords: regulatory compliance · assurance · knowledge modeling

1 Introduction

Establishing and assuring compliance with regulation can include both valuable and important activities for software-intensive companies. Regulation often contains demands for non-functional properties of software, whose purpose is to reduce the negative consequences that threaten business-, security- or safety-critical aspects of organizations and the wider society. In Europe, such demands are the result of deliberative legislative processes, and are meant to represent a legitimate, fair and equal deterrent against non-compliance. Assurance, defined

P. Bludau et al. (Eds.): SWQD 2024, LNBIP 505, pp. 135–152, 2024.
https://doi.org/10.1007/978-3-031-56281-5_8

as the *"justified confidence that the system functions as intended and is free of exploitable vulnerabilities"* [1], is thus paramount for information systems compliance and the success of software-intensive companies in the EU.

However, assuring compliance is still a very costly [2,3] problem area with continuously uncertain outcomes [4]. Among numerous challenges, we emphasize one core challenge: There is **no common language** that connects the **legal, organizational and technical knowledge** with corresponding **measures**. Regulation includes a very large and ambiguous body of laws that one must comply with, resulting in many viable strategies for compliance. It is often up to each organization to figure out a strategy based on their system and ecosystem, which is neither a trivial task nor guaranteed to satisfy what the law requires. Compliance-related activities are often separate from business activities, so technical measures are assured a posteriori without connections to the design and implementation.

This paper describes the efforts and particular challenges of a **European financial corporation in assuring compliance of software assets and business processes** with security-oriented regulatory demands. In particular, we address the question: *What are the challenges to assuring compliance of heterogeneous software systems, roles and processes with interpreted regulatory demands?* We argue that these observed challenges underlie the costliness and uncertainty of main compliance efforts.

This paper is structured as follows. First, we describe the background (Sect. 2), research approach (Sect. 3) and observations (Sect. 4) of our qualitative action-oriented case study. With a focus on an annual audit, we explore the roles, knowledge and facets involved, and identify six challenges which hinder organizations in achieving situational awareness and gradually demonstrating compliance. Finally, we explore the implications of this diagnostic snapshot for the traditional setup of auditing and assurance (Sect. 5), briefly discussing potential avenues for resolving the compliance bottlenecks (Sect. 6).

2   Background

2.1   Regulation and Compliance

The following section defines regulation, compliance, and assurance for the purposes of case study description.

Regulation refers to both a process and an object. Regulation as a process refers to "intentional intervention in the activities of a target population (...) exercised by public-sector actors on the economic activities of private-sector actors" (p. 11, [5]). Regulation as an object refers to the results of that process, i.e., "binding legal norm created by a state organ that intends to shape the conduct of individuals and firms" (p. 6, [6]). cf. [5]). We use the term "regulation" to describe the object, i.e., the relevant body of legal rules, which also extends to their references to standards and similar documentation (cf. [7]).

Compliance refers both to the process of adhering to rules and the status of having done so successfully [8]. We focus on the process of regulatory compliance, and refer to what [9] call "rule statements" as demands. We distinguish demands from clear rules and requirements (which are terms [10] use to describe "compliance obligations"), since we observe in the case that these statements are often ambiguously formulated and far from good practice according to requirements engineering (cf. [11]). Proving compliance with demands is difficult, and even considered to be an NP-hard problem [12].

For the purpose of the paper, we refer to assurance as the process of establishing justifiable confidence based on evidence [1]. Auditing plays two dominant roles in assuring compliance, especially in software-intensive companies and security-critical issues [4,13] that are relevant to the case. First, organizations themselves design and implement compliance measures they think are required (with or without external help), and then perform regular internal checks to make sure the design stays implemented. Second, regulators designate external auditors who should be allowed to perform ad hoc checks, and report back to supervisory authorities to confirm or enforce compliance.

We consider the process of *assuring compliance* as containing three complementary approaches for establishing confidence: pre-, during and post-execution activities [12]. The first "compliance by design" approach is relatively novel, proposing that business processes and assets be modeled according to demands [14]. The second "compliance-in-runtime" approach implements predesigned continuous checks and handles deviations by event-based testing (cf. [15,16]). The third approach represents a traditional time-based audit (i.e., "compliance by detection"), which the previous approaches intend to substitute.

2.2   Role of Interpretation

Due to the known ambiguity of regulatory demands [11,17], compliance requires choosing interpretations. Regulatory interpretation has an established history (cf. [18]), including formal studies of case law [19] or recitals [20]. We refer to interpretations as any body of operationalized legal demands or rules for the purposes of the regulated [18]. More specifically, we focus on four rough categories (cf. Table 1) that are relevant to the context of our case in civil law systems of Europe, the financial industry and software-intensive organizations.

First, standards operationalize ambiguous demands into technical requirements and measures. Standards can often influence how law is defined, and become mandatory themselves [7,21], often directly influencing the compliance of safety- or security-critical software[1] across industries [22]. Second, recommendations and opinions provide legitimate exemplary strategies and measures that organizations can apply [23]. Published by legal, industry or technical experts, opinion can include analysis [24], best practices and procedural checklists [25], design patterns [26], and even specialized regulatory technology [27].

---

[1] For example, ISO 13485:2012 for software medical devices, ISO 15497:2000 for automotive software.

Third, direct expert advice can be provided by specialized consultants [28], service providers [29], and internal roles. Advice operationalizes the demands in the context of the organization, often including a variety of internal business (e.g., compliance [30] or information security officers [31]) and engineering roles (e.g., security [32], privacy engineers [33]). Fourth, results of audits, inspections and certifications lead to new and validated measures over time. During audits, auditors provide a "proof" (i.e., a certificate or a report) of regulatory (non-)compliance to the regulated and/or the regulator, and help organizations generate legally validated knowledge and documents in iterations. Examples include process traditional audits, testing, attack simulations, or forensic investigations (cf. [34]).

Table 1. Sources of demands and their characteristics from the perspective of an organization.

Source	Legal status	Record	Operational to
Regulation	Binding	External	Political region
Standards	Case-based	External	Industry
Expert opinion	Non-binding	External	Industry, software
Expert advice	Non-binding	Internal	Organization
Audit	Case-based	Internal	Organization

2.3 Related Work

This section provides a non-exhaustive overview of related work that motivates this paper. Two studies provide primers into the problems of assuring compliance. [35] identify 15 industry challenges through interviews with compliance management experts in Australia. Their analysis delves into the general problems faced by compliance managers while working on audit-based assurance with the regulated, the regulations and technical solutions. [4] analyze the overarching challenge inherent in assuring compliance with information security standards, positing that the true security of the system cannot be completely assured with checklists, standard-driven compliance goals or external audits.

Two papers provide holistic representations of compliance processes, for the purpose of determining and resolving challenges. [12] perform a thorough tertiary survey of literature, reporting with an overview of the compliance problem and dominant solutions areas, and the challenges for roles working on explicating the logic of compliance and developing technical solutions for assurance. [36] instead use survey and interview data to express concepts and issues of general compliance management in a model, providing a general ontology that can be instantiated in a specified case. The solutions explored in these papers provide the ground for future action.

Other concepts relevant to this study include: compliance by design [14]; compliance in runtime [15,16]; assurance for information security [13]; regulatory demands on software quality [21,37]; and the interpretative nature of compliance [38,39].

3 Research Approach

3.1 Description of the Industrial Case

The following section describes the case. Our case centers on a large multinational financial corporation, headquartered in Europe, whose business focuses on a range of financial infrastructural services. The organization's work is deeply digital, spanning several lines of B2B and B2C services and twenty (compliance-relevant) software assets, half of which have been fully internally developed. The organization is in the midst of a digital transformation initiative that will establish a platform to unify the software processes and assets underlying the provision of these services.

A large part of this transformation includes establishing *compliance by design* across the entire corporation. This mostly includes remodeling software and associated processes to be directly related and compliant with regulatory demands on quality properties (cf. [40]), rarely involving new software assets, processes or functional non-software properties[2]. This effort is distributed across clusters of teams and their assets and processes (e.g., auditing at different levels, know-your-customer checks), leading to several interdependent subcases under the governance and security umbrellas. As of December 2023, four subcases are being actively researched: performing end-of-year IT security-centric audits; unifying identity and access management procedures; implementing the findings of an in-depth IT audit; and optimizing know-your-X onboarding processes. The order and intensity in which they are covered is driven by the needs and capacities of the involved teams.

At the current stage of case exploration, the regulatory ecosystem of the organization involves three national and EU laws and their dependencies, with demands for information security, IT governance, or digital mechanisms that reduce the risk of financial misconduct. As shown in the examples in Table 2, interpretations play a crucial role in establishing links between ambiguous terminology of laws and actual information security measures.

In the course of research presented in this paper, we focus on the 2022 and 2023 end-of-year audits as a tangible example of a complex, iterative and legally binding activity. Each audit is performed by an external auditor, lasting months and involving at least several dozen employees across the corporation. The predominant focus of these audits is on the security-centric quality demands that approximately 20 software assets and their processes must fulfill. Topics

---

[2] We suspect that software-relevant regulation is dominantly concerned with software quality as defined by [40], but we limit the scope of our claims to the case itself.

include: role- and purpose-based confidentiality of information (e.g., "need-to-know" access controls and recertification); security of networks, software supply chains and modules; compartmentalization and separation of concerns; traceability and automated verifiability via logs; and usage controls and transparency (e.g., four-eyes principle).

Table 2. Sources, items and texts of example demands in the explored regulatory-interpretive ecosystem.

Source	Item	Demand
Regulation	Digital Operational Resilience Act [41]	Art. 8, para. 4 (c): "financial entities shall (...) implement policies that limit the physical and virtual access to ICT system resources"
Standards	ISAE 3402 [42]	pp. 148: "a control is operating effectively if (...) it provides reasonable assurance that material misstatements, whether due to fraud or error, are prevented, or detected and corrected"
Expert opinion	Software service requirements	Multifactor authentication is required, single sign-on is optional
Expert advice	Spreadsheet for annual audits	Potential measure: Security configuration preferences policy with explanations
Audit	Report from a deep audit	"All user accounts must be deactivated for employees who have already left"

3.2   Research Methodology

We are engaged in research activities on compliance with the corporation since March 2021. Our task is to iteratively study the compliance-relevant processes and assets, represent the knowledge by modeling, and reason through potential solutions with the organizational stakeholders. Therefore, we have access to every required IS, including documents, softwares and processes. This unique access to empirical data is accompanied by interviews with owners of the correspondings assets as well as internal and external subject matter experts such as auditors.

The main goal of the project is to remodel and evaluate existing measures, and establish new ones, for proactive, near real-time awareness of compliance (further: *compliance measures*). Thus, in this case study, we are involved as both observers and actors in a combination of case study research [43] and action research [44]. This combined paradigm is applicable for studying both "what practitioners say [and] what practitioners actually do" (p. 96, [46]), and co-designing potential solutions to be tested [44]. It involves an iterative sequence of research and action at the level of a subcase, wherein we collect and analyze information in the first phase, and then provide models, recommendations and prototypical examples for validation and future actions in the second phase (cf. [44,45]). In this paper, we illustrate only the results of research and modeling, before recommendations are adopted.

The case study is of a qualitative and mixed-methods nature. Data collection involves a mixture of all three degrees of sources [43], namely: documents, observations, interviews, and workshops. These are discussed in turn. The modeling method of analysis that unifies information from the sources is covered in the next subsection.

Accessed documents can be classified as standalone files (i.e., mostly qualitative archival data) and content accessible via software-specific user interfaces. Shared standalone files include spreadsheets (e.g., risk analyses, auditing spreadsheets), official company documents (e.g., policies, presentations), diagrams, log files, and on occasion, emails, source code and documentation. Other content has been accessed via enterprise content management, issue-tracking, and access management systems, as well as other specialized software assets used or referred to in compliance activities. Observations were conducted in online corporate meetings with external auditors, and meetings between the GRC and business-line teams. In these settings, our role has been that of a case 3 observer [43] who does not participate directly in the auditing or other work, but whose presence is acknowledged by the research subjects. Intersections with other methods occur when interactions in emails, or detailed process and software walkthroughs in workshops, are observed.

Since May 2023, we have continuously been conducting interviews with the members of the *IT Governance, Risk and Compliance* (GRC) and three business-line teams, on a biweekly basis. At first interview, interviewees are made aware of the action-oriented research approach. Based on the progress of each subcase, we alternate between unstructured deep-dives into a particular topic, and semi-structured interviews where content is defined from the analysis and in the meeting agenda. Interviews with multiple team members provide a way to triangulate the discussed details of compliance activities, such as, e.g., the effort needed to review audit-relevant logs.

Three day-long semi-structured workshops have been organized with multiple members of the GRC team in July, September, and October of 2023. Workshops allow us to collect additional details and validate the analyses. Although interviews and workshops are not recorded for confidentiality reasons, content is noted down during meetings, and analyzed by modeling [47] the coded concepts following the interview coding best practices of [43, 48].

3.3 Modeling

To understand the problem area, we analyze the data from different sources by modeling the entire information system and its ecosystem. Modeling is a method for representing the information collected from different sources as a semantic network of concepts, their connections and other properties. This method extends traditional analyses of coding interviews and documents [48] by linking the coded information in subject-predicate-object statements (i.e., semantic triples), and adding metadata such as the source or date obtained. The resulting sets of triples form a graph structure, thus composing the model of the case-relevant "world" which can be visualized, validated with stakeholders, and used for generation of hypotheses [43]. For a discussion of the benefits of analysis through modeling, see [49], for example.

Our approach follows state-of-the-art methods in knowledge representation literature, including ontology engineering and learning from text and data (cf., e.g., [47,50]). We adhere to RDF [51] and OWL2 [52] standards for defining triples in ontological models, but we represent data, documents and noted verbal information in their original format. Thus, the resulting compliance-relevant concepts (assets, processes, roles, quality characteristics or properties) are extracted in the original vocabulary of the domain. We use open access tools such as Stanford Protege [53] for freehand modeling, Ontotext Refine [54] for modeling from data, and store the resulting ontologies in a graph database (Ontotext GraphDB [55]). These ontologies are annotated, validated and triangulated in workshops and interviews with stakeholders, whereby each version is updated with evidence or a point-of-view, akin to the "basic ontological logs" in literature (i.e., "ologs" [49]).

4   Findings

4.1   Stakeholder Groups, Knowledge and Facets

Challenges occur in the context of interactions between the involved stakeholders. We observe four stakeholder groups that work on establishing and assuring compliance (cf. Table 3): **auditors** who investigate the business on behalf of the regulator; the **owners** and **developers** who are responsible for cultivating a business process or asset; and **compliance officers** who are the central interface between the two. Other stakeholders, such as the regulator who receives the audit results, or the external expert who provides opinion and advice, are not directly involved. We exclude them for the purpose of this analysis.

We use stakeholder groups to explain the shared functions of particular roles in the audit, while retaining the confidentiality of business information. Whereas auditors are a well-known group, we distinguish between the following groups that can nonetheless overlap:

- **Owners** largely represent heads, leaders and architects of software teams for, e.g., IT reliability, security, client infrastructure, data or enterprise services.
- **Developers** represent software developers, engineers, testers, or administrators of those same teams.
- **Compliance officers** refer to the GRC team in this example, but we argue for broader use of the term to include other internal technical (e.g., privacy engineers, quality assurance engineers) and process-oriented roles (e.g., compliance officer, data privacy officers; cf. [33]).

Table 3. Compliance-relevant knowledge needs and facets of each stakeholder group. Italicized facets are not shared with other groups.

Stakeholder	Needed knowledge	Facets
Auditor	downstream interpretations; design and implementation; tests of effectiveness; paths to evidence	evaluation of compliance and *generation of holistic report*; provision of evidence; design of compliance measures; *procedure and topic of audit*
Compliance Officer	up- and downstream intepretations; all demands; responsibilities and status; paths to evidence	evaluation of compliance; business assets and processes; provision of evidence; design of compliance measures; *policy content design*
Process/Asset Owner	up- and downstream interpretations; procedures and deadlines; relevant demands	business assets and processes; provision of evidence; design of compliance measures; *technical translation of demands*
Process/Asset Developer	upstream interpretation; relevant tasks	business assets and processes; design and *implementation* of compliance measures

The observed flow of information between stakeholder groups is structured hierarchically, as shown in Fig. 1. To establish situational awareness and make appropriate decisions, each group needs specific compliance-relevant knowledge and shared or unique access to facets[3] of compliance. In the observed case, knowledge is requested and shared via email, calls and meetings; embedded in text documents, spreadsheets, diagrams and webpages; and stored in various shared on-premise and cloud solutions.

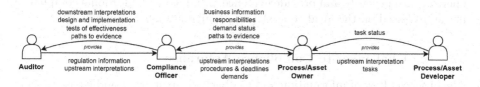

Fig. 1. Observed flow of information between stakeholders.

The following is an overview of observed and declared functions of each group. **Auditors** provide several spreadsheets with a predefined structure and prefilled columns, to help compliance officers organize audit-relevant information in the columns with empty cells. Prefilled columns contain the text, references and interpreted questions of a demand, and legally validated examples of potential

---

[3] Facet is a "hierarchy of homogeneous terms describing an aspect of the domain" (pp. 59, [56]). We include the view, tools, objects and rights to the facet.

compliance measures and appropriate evidence. In turn, to generate a holistic report, auditors need the compliance officers to insert information in the columns with empty cells: the claims about the design, implementation and effectiveness [42] of chosen compliance measures (i.e., downstream interpretations); and links and access to the appropriate evidence proving the claims. From interviews, we understand that auditors monitor the procedural aspects of the audit and yearly focus topics separately.

Compliance officers co-evaluate compliance of the entire organization by using knowledge from both upstream (i.e., regulation and intepretations) and downstream (relevant business information, responsibilities, technical measures) sources. They use the provided spreadsheets as both a checklist, and an editable distributed map showing the links between the demanded and actual compliance measures. Compliance officers delegate and orchestrate the provision of evidence, further translating the auditor's interpretations, where needed. We also observe that compliance officers reuse and restructure the auditor's prefilled information when preparing, evaluating and designing measures outside the auditing period.

Owners and **developers** need to understand only the domain-relevant demands, procedures, deadlines, and upstream interpretations. Although information from upstream sources includes technical language (e.g., *multifactor authentication*), the owner herself must translate them into the local context (e.g., *multifactor authentication via a dedicated app for single sign-on*), and develop specific technical tasks for developers to implement (e.g., *integrate software assets into the dedicated app for single sign-on*). The translation and design of compliance measures are parallel and back-and-forth activities between compliance officers, owners, and developers, with internal policies, webpages and domain expertise as reference points. As a result, owners and developers help compliance officers (or higher level owners) to fill in information in designated rows, and provide the evidence in a shareable cloud file system. Owners designate tasks for developers as issues stored on an agile DevOps software tool, and developers in turn generate and provide evidence, or implement additional compliance measures based on the local context (e.g., available tools or guidelines).

4.2   Six Challenges to Compliance Assurance

The observed flow of information and feedback illustrate that audit-based assurance poses six challenges to all stakeholder groups. Given their core responsibility to assure compliance before, during and after each audit, compliance officers are especially affected. The challenges themselves crystalized from the models of observed preparation of evidence and auditing meetings, auditing spreadsheets, documentary evidence, and the discussions with the GRC team.

C1: Very Large Number of Items and Mappings. Audits inherently involve a large number of items and mappings. Although the explored case centers on three laws, we number more than 700 individual paragraphs that have to be broken down and linked with compliance measures in the existing information system. In the annual audit, there are many-to-many mappings between approximately 100 paragraphs of one law and 100 examples of potential evidence for each of the 20 software applications. Most applications have at least two owners who designate (or occasionally perform) tasks, involving an unknown number of downstream owners and developers whose changes are logged in ticketing systems and version control tools.

C2: Unclear and Implicit Mappings. The mapping process is often effort- and interaction-intensive, but its results remain largely implicit. Auditors represent demands, potential measures and evidence as side-by-side lists, and other stakeholders fill in the adjacent cells with lists of claims and evidence. Observations and feedback show that this provides an incomplete picture for three reasons. First, lengths and structures of lists in adjacent cells do not necessarily match, so each reader must determine which items are linked and how. Even if lists are filled and sorted to match, the truncated text in cells obfuscates what is exactly claimed, how the claim satisfies the demand, or how and which parts of listed evidence prove that. Second, the items are not conceptually equivalent to each other, containing hidden many-to-many relationships: one demand can link to multiple measures; one measure can satisfy multiple demands, and represent multiple options across software applications; and an item of evidence can represent one or more files stored in one or more directories. We observe that compliance officers attempt to make the links explicit by restructuring the data and elaborating with metadata, but often do so in separate implicitly linked tables for readability reasons.

C3: Siloing of Knowledge. We observe that functional isolation of stakeholders creates a need for back-and-forth translations due to three knowledge siloes. First, owners and developers cultivate software applications, creating their own context-specific vocabulary adapted to their domain and business needs. Second, as audits require dedicated attention and orchestration, auditors and compliance officers inadvertently create compliance-specific vocabulary and documentation. Third, departure of individuals and infrequency of audits makes implicitly represented knowledge difficult to re-infer. Stakeholders recognize this challenge, and build stores of documentation (i.e., wikis) about previous audits. However, this need for further translation results in an increasing number of items that interpret the link between one law paragraph and an evidence file.

C4: Multiple Sources of Truth. Shared spreadsheets serve as the observed reference point of the audit, but observations and feedback show that no role can determine the status of compliance of the entire information system. Global status is tracked by aggregating "complete" cells, whose completeness is determined implicitly in helper columns. Local status, however, is visible only to individual auditors and compliance officers who devote substantial effort to maintain separate, implicitly linked views of each piece of the information system. Information is written from memory, or by copy-pasting texts, file names and file paths into tables and webpages. Changes (e.g., name, structure or content) and contradictions (e.g., negatively evaluated evidence, errors or missing values) can only be handled in the edited view. The result is that there are multiple static sources of truth, distributed across annotated pages and files, and indirectly oriented around an ambiguous checklist.

C5: High Costs of Audit-Based Learning. Learning from audits and potential compliance failure is very costly. Each annual audit results in several months of work for both auditors and compliance officers, alongside the substantial but unestimated effort for owners and developers. Interviews reveal that, for example, searching through evidence logs - one or few items in the context of the entire audit - costs an individual auditor more than 10 working days. Similarly, a compliance measure comprised of time-based recertification of employee access can cost each business team weeks of work. As compliance officers and owners acknowledge, when existing measures are insufficient, audits can result in new demands that take several years to implement despite the intention to comply. Until they are implemented, these intentions are stored in separate views or items (e.g., diagrams, tables, issues and tickets) that serve as intermediate reference material.

C6: Uncertain and Unintegrated Results of Traditional Auditing. Compliance checks and audits are low in frequency. However, they can also be inconclusive and thus difficult to integrate with all compliance activities in two ways. First, the validation of the auditor comes in the form of incremental verbal conclusions and a final report. A proof of compliance is an annual snapshot of a limited evaluation of heterogeneous claims and evidence. Unlike in formal proofs, the evidence itself comprises document, multimedia and other files with qualitative and quantitative content. Second, every attempt or request to map demands, claims and evidence results in substantial manual effort. Results of automatic (e.g., unit) tests or other audits with substantial evidence (e.g., penetration tests) comprise a small percentage of the annual audit. We observe that even in such automated or complete processes, there is a need for manual reinterpretation and repackaging into documentary evidence for the annual audit.

5   Discussion

5.1   Implications of Challenges

The combination of the identified six challenges hinders companies from assuring regulatory compliance with efficiency and certainty. Given that most measures deal with security-critical issues, we argue that three main implications make the resolution of these challenges important to all software-driven organizations.

In the following, we discuss implication and potential remedies for the presented challenges **C1-C6**.

First, we argue that the size (C1), distribution (C3-4) and established practice (C6) of compliance activities precede confusion (C2) and risk (C5). With many documents and multiple sources of truth, it is difficult to establish a full static picture of how compliant information systems are. Annual audits show that, without substantial external help and extensive effort to make knowledge explicit and integrated, compliance teams cannot reason about the (legal) purpose of information security measures, or infer new requirements from (legally or otherwise critically) insufficient protection. This is the original pain point of compliance-by-detection [14], for which clear traceability and a single point of truth may be first remedies.

Second, the dynamic nature of business, software, and compliance remain deeply unaddressed in assurance activities (cf. [35,57]). Although the organization accumulates stored knowledge, we observe that stakeholders remain disoriented with each change and yearly audit (C5). Compliance officers need to continuously refer back to previous audits and mappings to understand how a new compliance activity or business change affects the legal or general security of the organization (C2). Similarly, owners and developers cannot stably predict when business and compliance should be prioritized, but also struggle to implement new demands without first diagnosing how they may affect their systems and dependencies. We believe that filtered transparency and trace can enable roles to verify compliance of new actions continuously.

Third, while the interpretive role of auditors and compliance officers is valuable (cf. [38,39]), there is an overreliance on translation with an arbitrary and inconsistent purpose. The hierarchically flowing information is rarely immediately usable by other stakeholders, but we observe that frequent back-and-forth translation creates reiterated demands, claims and evidence whose purpose is potentially arbitrary. This results in loss of clarity and independence for developing strategies and assuring compliance in the local case. We believe that semantically interoperable and integrated facets can provide direct links between laws and evidence, thereby pruning strictly unnecessary translations.

5.2   Limitations

We find three apparent limitations of the study. First, the combination of research and action contains a potential threat to validity [45], such that there is a risk of actions biasing the research. We acknowledge that risk in our work, and understand the limited extensibility with respect to a purely observational and unseen role. To mitigate any potential bias, we separate the first phase findings of analyzed observations, documents and similar (i.e., case study research), from the planning, execution and evaluation of action in the second phase [45]. In all subcases, the action phase is still in the early stages, such that any recommendations following the identified challenges have not been implemented in the compliance activities. Additionally, we make our predefined role as researchers explicit to all teams, and emphasize that any future prototypical implementation is meant for further study.

Second, the scope of case and its subcases limits the extensibility of the findings. This particular study provides a snapshot of legally binding compliance activities in an information system of an EU-based multinational financial corporation. Thus, it does not cover experiences in other industries, countries or organizational types, nor demands from other sources. Similarly, the case involves experienced parties who recognize and accept the importance of compliance, and cooperate with each other to achieve it. We recognize the difference from parties whose non-compliance and contradictions are intentional or due to inexperience. Conclusions may not apply in their entirety to other settings.

Finally, conclusions from mixed-source modeling of the domain will differ from other approaches. The models reflect the world as determined by the collected data; we dedicate efforts to triangulate the concepts and their links, but acknowledge that models still represent abstractions of reality based on particular views. Conclusions from surveys, experimental or deductive studies, for example, likely differ. Similarly, modeling with strict metamodels (e.g., BPMN; [58]) may lead to analytical differences from modeling in domain ontologies. We invite researchers to deepen the understanding of the challenges with different methods of analysis and modeling.

6   Conclusion

We identify six challenges for assuring regulatory compliance from a qualitative industrial case study. By studying and modeling the information system of a European financial corporation and their audit-driven processes, we present an analysis of the involved stakeholder groups, knowledge and their facets. Focusing on the example of end-of-year audits, we illustrate the categories of commonly observed challenges, and argue that they contain direct implications for the cost of assurance and risk of non-compliance.

Future work centers on both research and action. Regarding research, compliance activities in further subcases will be studied more deeply, including know-your-X processes and the implementation of access controls and larger audit findings. Furthermore, other cases such as assuring compliance of artificial intelligence-driven IS will serve as strong ground for evaluating and extending the results in different contexts.

Regarding action, two avenues of future work show promise, which we intend to pursue. First, we argue that traceability, auditable transparency, and semantic interoperability will be core qualities of any prototypical solution. To achieve these properties, we investigate the use of assurance argumentation for compliance [59], with methods that enable the continuous integration of dynamic and diverse software, knowledge, and facets (cf. [60,61]). Second, we explore new auditing paradigms that retain the advantages of deep audits, while emphasizing compliant-by-design software architecture [62], and continuous handling of counterclaims and deviations in runtime [15,16]. These areas will hopefully demonstrate that compliance can be efficiently and confidently assured.

Acknowledgments. This work was partially supported by financial and other means by the following research projects: DUCA (EU grant agreement 101086308), FinComp (industrial research grant with no conflict of interest), FLA (funded by the Bavarian Ministry of Economics). We would also like to thank to all of the participants in interviews and workshops in the course of empirical data collection. Furthermore, we thank the four reviewers for comments and support.

Disclosure of Interests. The authors have no competing interests to declare that are relevant to the content of this article.

References

1. National Institute of Standards and Technology (NIST): Cybersecurity Supply Chain Risk Management Practices for Systems and Organizations. NIST Special Publication. NIST, Gaithersburg, MD
2. European Banking Authority (EBA): Study of the Cost of Compliance with Supervisory Reporting Requirements. Report EBA/Rep/2021/15. Luxembourg, EBA
3. Hammond, S., Cowan, M.: Cost of Compliance: Shaping the Future. Thomson Reuters Regulatory Intelligence, Toronto (2021)
4. Duncan, B., Whittington, M.: Compliance with standards, assurance and audit: does this equal security? In: ACM International Conference Proceeding Series, pp. 77–84, September 2014
5. Koop, C., Lodge, M.: What is regulation? An interdisciplinary concept analysis. Regul. Gov. **11**(1), 95–108 (2015)
6. Orbach, B.: What is regulation? Yale J. Regul. **30**(1), 1–10 (2012)
7. Balta, D., Krcmar, H.: Managing standardization in eGovernment: a coordination theory based analysis framework. In: Parycek, P., et al. (eds.) EGOV 2018. LNCS, vol. 11020, pp. 60–72. Springer, Cham (2018). https://doi.org/10.1007/978-3-319-98690-6_6
8. Sutinen, J.G., Kuperan, K.: A socio-economic theory of regulatory compliance. Int. J. Soc. Econ. **26**(1/2/3), 174–193 (1999)
9. Breaux, T.D., Vail, M.W., Anton, A.I.: Towards regulatory compliance: extracting rights and obligations to align requirements with regulations. In: 14th IEEE International Requirements Engineering Conference (RE 2006), Minneapolis and St. Paul, MN, 11–15 September, pp. 49–58 (2006)
10. International Organization for Standardization (ISO): ISO 37301:2021. Compliance management systems. Requirements with guidance for use. ISO, Geneva
11. Massey, A.K., Rutledge, R.L., Anton, A.I., Swire, P.P.: Identifying and classifying ambiguity for regulatory requirements. In: Proceedings of the 2014 IEEE 22nd International Requirements Engineering Conference (RE 2014), pp. 83–92 (2014)
12. Hashmi, M., Governatori, G., Lam, H.P., Wynn, M.T.: Are we done with business process compliance: state of the art and challenges ahead (2018)
13. Bozkus Kahyaoglu, S., Caliyurt, K.: Cyber security assurance process from the internal audit perspective. Manag. Account. J. **33**(4), 360–376 (2018)
14. Lohmann, N.: Compliance by design for artifact-centric business processes. Inf. Syst. **38**(4), 606–618 (2013)
15. Gomez-Lopez, M.T., Gasca, R.M., Perez-Alvarez, J.M.: Compliance validation and diagnosis of business data constraints in business processes at runtime. Inf. Syst. **48**, 26–43 (2015)

16. Awad, A., Barnawi, A., Elgammal, A., Elshawi, R., Almalaise, A., Sakr, S.: Runtime detection of business process compliance violations: an approach based on anti patterns? In: Proceedings of the 30th Annual ACM Symposium on Applied Computing (SAC 2015), Salamanca, Spain, 13–17 April, pp. 1203–1210 (2015)
17. Poscher, R.: Ambiguity and vagueness in legal interpretation. In: Tiersma, P., Solan, L. (eds.) The Oxford Handbook of Language and Law, Oxford University Press, Oxford (2011)
18. Randolph, G.M., Fetzner, J.P.: Regulatory interpretation: regulators, regulated parties, and the courts. Bus. Polit. **20**(2), 301–328 (2017)
19. Ponzetto, G.A.M., Fernandez, P.A.: Case law versus statute law: an evolutionary comparison. J. Leg. Stud. **37**(2), 379–430 (2008)
20. Klimas, T., Vaiciukaite, J.: The law of recitals in European community legislation. ILSA J. Int. Comp. Law **15**(1), 61–93 (2008)
21. Kempe, E., Massey, A.K.: Regulatory and security standard compliance throughout the software development lifecycle. In: Proceedings of the 54th Annual Hawaii International Conference on System Sciences, Virtual, 4–8 January, pp. 2026–2035 (2021)
22. Bujok, A.B., MacMahon, S.T., McCaffery, F., Whelan, D., Mulcahy, B., Rickard, W.J.: Safety critical software development – extending quality management system practices to achieve compliance with regulatory requirements. In: Clarke, P.M., O'Connor, R.V., Rout, T., Dorling, A. (eds.) SPICE 2016. CCIS, vol. 609, pp. 17–30. Springer, Cham (2016). https://doi.org/10.1007/978-3-319-38980-6_2
23. Yulianto, S., Lim, C., Soewito, B.: Information security maturity model: a best practice driven approach to PCI DSS compliance. In: Proceedings of the 2016 IEEE Region 10 Symposium (TENSYMP 2016), Bali, 9–11 May, pp. 65–70 (2016)
24. Humphreys, L., Santos, C., Di Caro, L., Boella, G., Van Der Torre, L., Robaldo, L.: Mapping recitals to normative provisions in EU legislation to assist legal interpretation. In: JURIX 2015: The Twenty-Eighth Annual Conference, Braga, Portugal, 10–11 December (2015). Frontiers Artif. Intell. Appl. **279**, 41–49
25. Floridi, L., Holweg, M., Taddeo, M., Silva, J.A., Mökander, J., Wen, Y.: capAI - a procedure for conducting conformity assessment of AI systems in line with the EU artificial intelligence act. SSRN. https://dx.doi.org/10.2139/ssrn.4064091
26. Hjerppe, K., Ruohonen, J., Leppanen, V.: The general data protection regulation: requirements, architectures, and constraints. In: Proceedings of the 27th IEEE International Conference on Requirements Engineering (RE2019), Jeju Island, 23–27 September, pp. 265–275 (2019)
27. Commission Nationale de l'Informatique et des Libertés (CNIL): The open source PIA software helps to carry out data protection impact assessment. https://www.cnil.fr/en/open-source-pia-software-helps-carry-out-data-protection-impact-assessment. Accessed 20 Nov 2023
28. Dzienkowski, J.S.: The future of big law: alternative legal service providers to corporate clients. Fordham Law Rev. **82**(6), 2995–3040 (2014)
29. Christensen, M., Skaerbaek, P.: Consultancy outputs and the purification of accounting technologies. Acc. Organ. Soc. **35**(5), 524–545 (2010)
30. Freeman, E.H.: Regulatory compliance and the chief compliance officer. Inf. Syst. Secur. **16**(6), 357–361 (2007)
31. Karanja, E.: The role of the chief information security officer in the management of IT security. Inf. Comput. Secur. **25**(3), 300–329 (2017)
32. Massacci, F., Prest, M., Zannone, N.: Using a security requirements engineering methodology in practice: the compliance with the Italian data protection legislation. Comput. Stand. Interfaces **27**(5), 445–455 (2005)

33. Klymenko, A., Meisenbacher, S., Matthes, F.: The structure of data privacy compliance. In: CIISR 2023: 3rd International Workshop on Current Information Security and Compliance Issues in Information Systems Research, 18 September 2023, Paderborn, Germany, pp. 85–91 (2023)
34. Moeller, R.: IT Audit, Control, and Security. Wiley, Hoboken, NJ (2010)
35. Abdullah, N.S., Sadiq, S., Indulska, M.: Emerging challenges in information systems research for regulatory compliance management. In: Proceedings of the International Conference on Advanced Information Systems Engineering (CAiSE 2010), pp. 251–265 (2010)
36. Abdullah, N.S., Indulska, M., Sadiq, S.: Compliance management ontology - a shared conceptualization for research and practice in compliance management. Inf. Syst. Front. 18(5), 995–1020 (2016)
37. Klymenko, O., Kosenkov, O., Meisenbacher, S., Elahidoost, P., Mendez, D., Matthes, F.: Understanding the implementation of technical measures in the process of data privacy compliance: a qualitative study. In: ESEM 2022, Helsinki, Finland, 19–23 September, pp. 261–271 (2022)
38. Lenglet, M.: Ambivalence and ambiguity: the interpretive role of compliance officers. In: Huault, I., Richard, C. (eds.) Finance: The Discreet Regulator, pp. 59–84. Palgrave Macmillan UK, London (2012). https://doi.org/10.1057/9781137033604_4
39. Chandler, D.: Organizational susceptibility to institutional complexity: critical events driving the adoption and implementation of the ethics and compliance officer position. Organ. Sci. 25(6), 1722–1743 (2014)
40. Chen, L., Babar, M.A., Nuseibeh, B.: Characterizing architecturally significant requirements. IEEE Softw. 30(2), 38–45 (2013)
41. European Commission: Proposal for a Regulation of the European Parliament and of the Council on digital operational resilience for the financial sector and amending Regulations (EC) No 1060/2009, (EU) No 648/2012, (EU) No 600/2014 and (EU) No 909/2014. Brussels, European Commission. https://eur-lex.europa.eu/legal-content/EN/TXT/?uri=CELEX%3A52020PC0595. Accessed 25 Oct 2023
42. International Auditing and Assurance Standards Board (IAASB): International Standard on Assurance Engagements (ISAE) 3402. Assurance Reports on Controls at a Service Organization, IAASB, New York, NY
43. Runeson, P., Höst, M.: Guidelines for conducting and reporting case study research in software engineering. Empir. Softw. Eng. 14, 131–164 (2009)
44. Sein, M.K., Henfridsson, O., Purao, S., Rossi, M., Lindgren, R.: Action design research. MIS Q. 35(1), 37–56 (2011)
45. Coughlan, P., Coghlan, D.: Action research for operations management. Int. J. Oper. Prod. Manag. 22(2), 220–240 (2002)
46. Avison, D.E., Lau, F., Myers, M.D., Nielsen, P.A.: Action research. Commun. ACM 42(1), 94–97 (1999)
47. Keet, C.M.: The What and How of Modelling Information and Knowledge: From Mind Maps to Ontologies. Springer, Cham (2023). https://doi.org/10.1007/978-3-031-39695-3
48. Yin, R.K.: Case Study Research and Applications. Design and Methods, 6th edn. Sage Publications, Los Angeles, CA (2017)
49. Spivak, D.I., Kent, R.E.: Ologs: a categorical framework for knowledge representation. PLoS ONE 7(1), 1–22 (2012)
50. Watrobski, J.: Ontology learning methods from text - an extensive knowledge-based approach. Procedia Comput. Sci. 176. Proceedings of the 24th KES International

Conference on Knowledge-Based and Intelligent Information and Engineering Systems (KES 2020), Virtual, 16–18 September, pp. 3356–3368 (2020)

51. World Wide Web Consortium (W3C): RDF/XML Syntax Specification (Revised). https://www.w3.org/TR/REC-rdf-syntax/. Accessed 25 Oct 2023

52. World Wide Web Consortium (W3C): OWL 2 Web Ontology Language. RDF-Based Semantics, 2nd Edn. https://www.w3.org/TR/owl2-rdf-based-semantics/. Accessed 25 Oct 2023

53. Musen, M.A.: The Protégé project: a look back and a look forward. AI Matters **1**(4), 4–12 (2015)

54. Ontotext: Ontotext Refine Overview and Features. https://platform.ontotext.com/ontorefine/. Accessed 25 Oct 2023

55. Ontotext: What is GraphDB? https://graphdb.ontotext.com/documentation/10.4/. Accessed 25 Oct 2023

56. Giunchiglia, F., Dutta, B., Maltese, V., Farazi, F.: A facet-based methodology for the construction of a large-scale geospatial ontology. J. Data Semant. **1**, 57–73 (2012)

57. Golumbic, C.E.: The big chill: personal liability and the targeting of financial sector compliance officers. Hastings Law J. **69**(1), 45–93 (2017)

58. Object Management Group (OMG): Business Process Model and Notation (BPMN). OMG, Milford, MA. https://www.omg.org/spec/BPMN/2.0/PDF. Accessed 25 Oct 2023

59. Bloomfield, R., Rushby, J.: Assessing Confidence with Assurance 2.0. CSL Technical Report SRI-CSR-2022. SRI International, Menlo Park, CA (2022)

60. Sunkle, S., Kholkar, D., Kulkarni, V.: Explanation of proofs of regulatory (Non-)compliance using semantic vocabularies. In: 9th International Web Rule Symposium (RuleML 2015), Berlin, Germany, 2–5 August, pp. 388–403 (2015)

61. Gallina, B., Olessen, T.Y., Parajdi, E., Aarup, M.: A knowledge management strategy for seamless compliance with the machinery regulation. In: Proceedings of the 30th European & Asian System, Software & Service Process Improvement & Innovation (EuroSPI 2023), pp. 220–234 (2023)

62. Sellami, M., Bueno Momcilovic, T., Kuhn, P., Balta, D.: Interaction patterns for regulatory compliance in federated learning. In: Proceedings of the 3rd International Workshop on Current Information Security and Compliance Issues in Information Systems Research, pp. 6–18 (2023)

A PUF-Based Approach for Copy Protection of Intellectual Property in Neural Network Models

Daniel Dorfmeister$^{(\boxtimes)}$, Flavio Ferrarotti , Bernhard Fischer ,
Martin Schwandtner , and Hannes Sochor

Software Competence Center Hagenberg, Softwarepark 32a, 4232 Hagenberg, Austria
{daniel.dorfmeister,flavio.ferrarotti,
bernhard.fischer,martin.schwandtner,hannes.sochor}@scch.at

Abstract. More and more companies' Intellectual Property (IP) is being integrated into Neural Network (NN) models. This IP has considerable value for companies and, therefore, requires adequate protection. For example, an attacker might replicate a production machines' hardware and subsequently simply copy associated software and NN models onto the cloned hardware. To make copying NN models onto cloned hardware infeasible, we present an approach to bind NN models—and thus also the IP contained within them—to their underlying hardware. For this purpose, we link an NN model's weights, which are crucial for its operation, to unique and unclonable hardware properties by leveraging Physically Unclonable Functions (PUFs). By doing so, sufficient accuracy can only be achieved using the target hardware to restore the original weights, rendering proper execution of the NN model on cloned hardware impossible. We demonstrate that our approach accomplishes the desired degradation of accuracy on various NN models and outline possible future improvements.

Keywords: neural networks · intellectual property protection · physically unclonable functions · hardware-software binding

1 Introduction

Neural Network (NN) models are increasingly deployed in all areas, including industry. For instance, they are readily applied for quality optimisation and process automation in diverse industrial machines. To make this possible, a considerable amount of resources, including time and money, are being invested in the development of NN models, which therefore increasingly incorporate the core Intellectual Property (IP) of companies. In this context, it is important to ensure the privacy of the training data of the models, i.e., to prevent the extraction of

The research reported in this paper has been funded by BMK, BMAW, and the State of Upper Austria in the frame of the COMET Module Dependable Production Environments with Software Security (DEPS) and the SCCH competence center INTEGRATE within the COMET - Competence Centers for Excellent Technologies Programme managed by Austrian Research Promotion Agency FFG.

P. Bludau et al. (Eds.): SWQD 2024, LNBIP 505, pp. 153–169, 2024.
https://doi.org/10.1007/978-3-031-56281-5_9

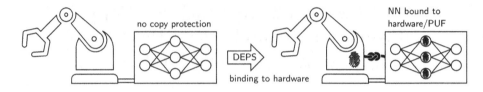

Fig. 1. Copy Protection: A NN model tied to a target machine.

the original data from the models. An important effort is indeed being made to deal with this problem (see, e.g., [11]).

However, a rather neglected aspect is the fact that NN models can be easily copied and used without due authorisation. This is known as software piracy and comprises the unauthorised copy, use, download, and distribution of software. In this sense, a pre-trained NN model is not different to classical software, beyond the fact that it is learned instead of programmed. We can differentiate among end-user, online and commercial piracy. End-user piracy occurs when the software lacks copy protection and end-users illegally redistribute it in their private circle. Online piracy is the distribution of pirated software online via a central server or a peer-to-peer file sharing platform. Commercial piracy refers to an organisation that pirates software to gain a financial advantage, mainly by counterfeiting and then reselling it as original software or as part of a product that uses this software. The main motivations for software piracy and their consequences for companies are well documented for a long time [14]. For all types of software piracy, the main problem is inadequate copy protection [4].

In an industrial setting, the lack of copy protection built into NNs means that it is often not even necessary to know anything about a NN model, but it is enough to simply make a copy of it in order to profit at the expense of the IP owner. In Germany alone, it is estimated that product or brand piracy accounts for an annual loss of 6.4 billion euros[1]. The main effort when stealing IP from production machines is primarily in reverse engineering and cloning the hardware, as software and NN models can be simply copied.

In this paper, we propose a possible solution to the described problem. Our solution differs from classical copy protection mechanisms, usually based on passwords or hardware dongles, as it is well known that they are rather easy to circumvent, and can also be expensive if done properly. We follow an approach based on binding a given NN model to a specific target machine so that its accuracy is reduced when copied (without authorisation) and used on a different machine. We choose a protection approach based on making the copied NN model inaccurate instead of straight out unusable, as it can make the protection less obvious and thus more difficult to break for an attacker. At the same time, this reduces the runtime overhead of authorised uses of the protected model.

---

[1] VDMA Study Product Piracy 2022 (https://www.vdma.org/documents/34570/51629660/VDMA+Study+Product+Piracy+2022_final.pdf).

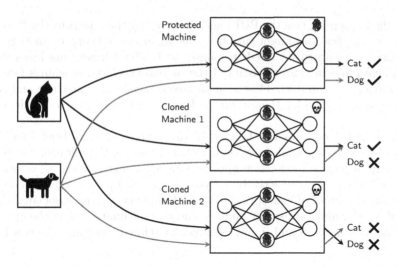

Fig. 2. Behaviour of copy protected NN model in target vs. cloned machines.

In order to achieve the binding between a NN model and a target machine, i.e., the machine where the model is authorised to run on, we must be able to uniquely identify the underlying hardware. In the project DEPS[2] (short for *Dependable Production Environments with Software Security*) we are exploring different ways of achieving precisely this objective. In particular, a promising approach to software-hardware binding is the use of Physically Unclonable Functions (PUFs), a hardware-based security primitive. This primitive arises from the fact that each circuit has unique physical properties resulting from unintended variations in the manufacturing process. Consequently, these physical properties function as a digital fingerprint that cannot be easily cloned, which is the basis for PUFs. PUFs can either use dedicated hardware or components already present in systems, such as DRAM.

Figure 1 illustrates this general idea: We have an industrial machine, e.g., a robot arm with a neural network-based adaptive control method for trajectory tracking [19]. To protect it from being copied and used without authorisation, a fingerprint is taken from the industrial machine and tied to the neural network. More precisely, several weights of the NN model are bound to the fingerprint in such a way that the NN model can only provide sufficient accuracy on the basis of this fingerprint. If such an industrial machine is now cloned and the protected NN model linked to the original hardware is copied to this cloned machine, the underlying fingerprint is now different and the NN model therefore no longer provides sufficient accuracy.

Figure 2 exemplifies the impact of our protection method on the accuracy of unauthorised copies of a NN model. The protected target machine classifies the pictures of a dog and a cat correctly, while the two pirated copies cannot

---

[2] https://deps.scch.at.

verify the fingerprint (via the PUF) and thus classify them incorrectly. Note that incorrect classifications might vary from one unauthorised copy to another. This is because the fingerprint (PUF response) will differ between machines due to the unique physical characteristics of the individual cloned machines (see, e.g., cloned machines 1 and 2). That is, if an adversary clones a machine and copies the protected NN model, then it will no longer work as reliable as on the target machine.

The paper is organised as follows: In the next section, we briefly introduce the necessary background on NNs and PUFs, and fix the notation. In Sect. 3, we specify the threat model assumptions. Our main contribution is condensed in Sects. 4–7 where we, respectively, introduce our novel protection mechanism, a corresponding proof of concept strategy and implementation, associated experimental results, and discuss our findings and current limitations of the approach. The final two Sects. 8 and 9, are reserved for related work and the conclusion, respectively.

2   Preliminaries

In this section, we provide the necessary background regarding neural network models and physically unclonable functions, and we fix the notation used throughout the paper.

2.1   Neural Networks

There are many different kinds of (artificial) Neural Networks (NNs) such as feed forward (a.k.a. multilayer perceptrons), recurrent, and convolutional NNs. All have in common that their architecture can be defined by some type of directed graph with a set of nodes V, set of edges $E \subseteq V \times V$ and functions $(a_v)_{v \in V}$, where for every node $v \in V$ (usually excluding the input nodes), $a_v : \mathbb{R} \to \mathbb{R}$ is a continuous function known as *activation function* at v. A concrete NN model associates this skeleton architecture with a *weight* $w_e \in \mathbb{R}$ with every edge $e \in E$ and a *bias* b_v with every node $v \in V$. NN models compute functions, but the way in which this is done varies depending on the type of NN used. A constant in this sense is that the computation takes place in the nodes and is propagated through the graph, using the activation functions, weights and biases. The weight and biases are learned from data. We are not concerned with the learning process itself but with protecting the IP produced by this process in the form of a pre-trained model. Thus, it make sense to encrypt the weights in the pre-trained model so that an adversary cannot simply copy and use it without permission.

2.2   Physically Unclonable Functions

A Physically Unclonable Function (PUF) f is a function defined using unique physically properties of hardware that cannot be cloned. Typically, it takes a binary string b as input (challenge) and returns a possibly different binary string

b' as output (response). For each binary string b in the domain of f, there is a corresponding $b' = f(b)$, which is unique for the hardware of the target machine M. More concretely, if f is a PUF, $f(b)$ will be interpreted at run-time as b' only if challenged on M. Otherwise, the response value $f(b)$ will be arbitrary, and it can be assumed that $f(b) \neq b'$ for almost all machines M' different from M.

There is a variety of PUFs that can be used in the context of the protection proposed in this paper. For instance, in our project DEPS, we are experimenting with DRAM PUFs [5], where the PUF response $f(b) = b'$ to a challenge b is the result of applying the Rowhammer exploit to flip some bits of b, which is predictable in certain locations of the target DRAM. Many other alternatives exist, e.g., arbiter PUFs, SRAM PUFs, ring oscillator PUFs, and optical PUFs [1, 10]. Any of these alternatives can be used for implementing the copy protection approach that we propose in this paper. The choice depends on the available PUFs for the hardware where the trained NN model will be used, as well as the response time and level of strength provided by the available options. This is application-specific and should be evaluated on a case by case basis.

3   Threat Model

In this paper, we only consider attacks that aim to remove the copy protection of the NN model, e.g., through reverse engineering. We assume that an attacker can gain access to a model, e.g., via an update mechanism, backup of the machine, or download of the firmware from the machine. We do not consider attacks on hardware such as side-channel attacks or other attack vectors, e.g., supply chain attacks. This also means that we are currently looking at a mere static attacker. This attacker has access to only the model and all the information it contains and can, therefore, not query the PUF and thus obtain Challenge-Response Pairs (CRPs). However, we assume that our encryption method is public knowledge, as security through obscurity would be bad practice. Both static and dynamic analysis are described below. The focus of protection against dynamic analysis is future work and will be discussed in Sect. 7.

3.1   Static Analysis

Using static analysis, an attacker does not execute the software—including NN models—to be analysed but has access to the binary, potentially also to the source code of the software. Thus, an attacker has access to all the information that is present while the program is not running.

For example, a piece of software uses an NN model and requires a key for decryption of the model's encrypted weights. If the key is incorrect, the model's weights are not decrypted correctly and, therefore, the model does not achieve sufficient accuracy. However, if the encryption key is hidden somewhere within the program, an attacker may find this key through static analysis, decrypt the model and thus gain access to the model.

Attacks based on static analysis are possible as long as all data that is needed to successfully run a program or model is contained within themselves. To counter such attacks, essential data must be inaccessible. An example would be to prompt a third party, e.g., the user or a PUF for the decryption key so it does not have to be part of the program or model anymore.

3.2 Dynamic Analysis

Dynamic analysis is based on observing the behaviour and state of a program or NN at runtime. This reaches from executing a program with various inputs and observing its behaviour from the outside by, e.g., dumping its memory, to employing a interactive disassembler. Interactive disassemblers enable the reverse engineer to analyse a program at any time during its execution using breakpoints and enables inspection of memory at any state.

Dynamic analysis enables an attacker to use data only present at runtime in addition to information available from static analysis. Suppose a cryptographic key is hidden successfully so that it cannot be retrieved by means of static analysis and it is also hidden at runtime. The instructions of the program have to be decrypted at some point while executing the program. However, an attacker can wait until each instruction has been decrypted at least once and can thus recover the full program. This also applies to NN. To successfully execute a NN, we must know the internal structure of the NN as well as its assigned weights. Whenever we need to perform some calculations using a weight, the correct, decrypted value must be provided.

In this work, we focus on protection against static analysis. Therefore, our goal is to remove critical information from the model and make it only available at runtime. Providing a sound method that prevents static analysis is a first step to secure NN models and already poses a significant challenge for attackers.

4 Copy Protection Method

The goal of our copy protection method is to prevent unauthorised copy and use of pre-trained NN models. We propose the use of PUFs (see Sect. 2.2) to encrypt some of the weights w_e associated with the edges $e \in E$ of an NN model, so that the model only works correctly on its target machine. If used on a different machine—even on a clone of the target machine—, the model will drop its accuracy to levels that are determined by the number and selection of encrypted weights. As we explained in Sect. 2.1, weights are learned from data and are a key IP asset contained in any pre-trained NN model, making them an ideal target for protection. The reader might ask why we encrypt just some of the weights and not all of them. The answer is that this way our method can limit the performance overhead caused by decryption and, as shown in this paper, still provide an adequate level of protection.

More concretely, given a NN model N with set of edges E and corresponding weights w_e for every $e \in E$, plus a PUF f with domain D_f for a target machine

M, we propose a protection method based on binding N to M (so that N only works correctly on M) via encryption/decryption of a subset of the weights of N using f. Before the encryption process starts, we need to decide the number n of weights from N that we want to encrypt. This number depends on various factors that are application specific. In particular, these are the desired drop in accuracy of N when used on unauthorised hardware and the performance overhead when used on the authorised hardware. We analyse this issue over some concrete NN models in Sect. 6.

For the encryption procedure, we adapt the well known one-time key encryption mechanics in the special form of Vernam [2, Section 13.2], using the PUF f (by selecting a challenge at random) to generate the cipher key. We work with the binary representation of the real-valued weights. Thus, we use $toBin(w_e) = b_e$ and $toFloat(b_e) = w_e$ to denote the binary representation b_e of weight w_e and its inverse function, respectively. We assume that the binary representation of a weight is of length m, i.e., $|toBin(w_e)| = m$ for all weight w_e of N. We further assume that the PUF f is challenged with binary strings of length m and responds with binary strings of the same length.

The method to copy protect N can be outlined as follows:

– The *weight selection* algorithm chooses a subset $S \subseteq E$ of edges of size $|S| = n$.
– For each weight w_e with $e \in S$, the *key generation* algorithm chooses a (challenge) $c_e \in D_f$ randomly.
– For each weight w_e with $e \in S$, the *encryption* algorithms handles the binary representation $toBin(w_e) = (w_{e1}, \ldots, w_{em})$ (the plaintext) and the PUF response $f(c_e) = (k_{e1}, \ldots k_{em})$ (the cipher key) as streams, and uses each corresponding pair of a plaintext bit w_{ei} and a cipher key bit c_{ei} as input for a XOR operation, yielding a ciphertext bit $p_{ei} = k_{ei} \oplus w_{ei}$.
– For each ciphertext (encrypted weight) $p_e = (p_{e1}, \ldots, p_{em})$, the *decryption* algorithm obtains the corresponding key using the PUF response $f(c_e) = (k_{e1}, \ldots k_{em})$ and treats each corresponding pair of a ciphertext bit p_{ei} and a cipher key bit k_{ei} as input for a XOR operation. Since

$$k_{ei} \oplus p_{ei} = k_{ei} \oplus (k_{ei} \oplus w_{ei}) = (k_{ei} \oplus k_{ei}) \oplus w_{ei} = 0 \oplus w_{ei} = w_{ei},$$

the XOR operation yields the original bit in the binary representation of w_e (i.e., the original plaintext bit). Finally, $toFloat(w_{e1}, \ldots, w_{em}) = w_e$.

Note that the use of the PUF f to retrieve the key means that decryption of the weights is correct only if the response to the challenges chosen during encryption is the one given by the PUF f on the target machine M. In case a hardware component the PUF is based on needs to be replaced, the NN model must be decrypted first an re-encrypted using the new hardware. Alternatively,—especially if the hardware component failed—the original, unencrypted model can be encrypted for the new hardware and re-deployed to the altered target machine.

5 Proof of Concept

As a Proof of Concept (PoC), we implemented the copy protection method for
NNs described in the previous section using Python 3.10 and TensorFlow 2.14.
The pseudocode in Listing 1 shows how our PoC implements the weight selection,
key generation and encryption.

```
1  def encrypt_model(model, layer_id, pct, data):
2    print "Accuracy = " + model.evaluate(data) # = 0.97
3    chosen_weights :=
4      choose_weights(model.layers[layer_id].weights, pct)
5
6    foreach weight_id in chosen_weights:
7      w := model.layers[layer_id].weights[weight_id]
8      choose challenge in domain(puf): # randomly
9        p := puf(challenge) xor w
10       model.layers[layer_id].weights[weight_id] := p
11       helper[weight_id] := challenge
12
13   save(helper, layer_id)
14   print "Accuracy = " + model.evaluate(data) # e.g., = 0.75
```

Listing 1: Encrypt model's weights (before NN deployment).

The algorithm encrypt_model takes the following parameters: the NN model
(model), the layer that we want to encrypt (layer_id), the percentage of weights
of a given layer that must be encrypted (pct), and input data (data) to test the
accuracy of the model with both the original and modified weights after the
encryption. Note that we use the layer for evaluation purposes since it is a
known fact that certain layers are more significant than others.

Our PoC starts by testing the accuracy of the model for classifying the inputs
in data (line 2), which is repeated once the model is encrypted (line 14) to test
the accuracy of the resulting model with modified (encrypted) weights. This way,
we can determine whether the given percentage of encrypted weights is sufficient
to degrade the model's responses, rendering unauthorised copies of the model
useless.

The subset of weights to be encrypted (chosen_weights) is randomly chosen from weights in the selected layer of the model, where the cardinality of
chosen_weights amounts to the percentage pct of all weights in that layer
(lines 3–4). By increasing pct, we can increase the strength of our protection, at
the cost of runtime overhead while encrypting and decrypting the model.

Next (lines 6–11), the key generation and encryption is performed for each
of the chosen weights. Note that we keep track of the corresponding challenge
for each weight_id using the helper vector. This is needed to recover the key

via the `puf` function when the encrypted weight `p` needs to be decrypted, which only works correctly on the target machine.

Currently, we use a simulated XOR arbiter PUF [16], implemented in the pypuf library[3]. This allows our PoC to work on any PC for demonstration purposes (as long as pypuf is installed). We can decide which machine's PUF responses we want to simulate by providing a seed to pypuf. In practice, we should of course use an actual PUF for the target machine, instead of a simulated one. Then, the model should be encrypted on the target machine using our algorithm in Listing 1, or alternatively by modifying the algorithm to use a database that maps PUF challenges to the target machine's responses.

```
def decrypt_model(model, data):
  helper, layer_id := load()

  foreach (weight_id, challenge) in helper:
    p := model.layers[layer_id].weights[weight_id]
    w := puf(challenge) xor p
    model.layers[layer_id].weights[weight_id] := w

  print "Accuracy = " + model.evaluate(data)
  # Accuracy = 0.97 (on target machine)
  # Accuracy < 0.97 (on cloned/different machine)
```

Listing 2: Decrypt model's weights (when executed on the target machine).

In Listing 2, we describe our corresponding PoC approach for decryption of weights of a given NN model. This procedure results in the correct model if, and only if, the PUF's responses to the required challenges coincide with the responses used during encryption. In turn, this should only happen in practice if the decryption algorithm is run on the target machine. For added security against static attacks, we propose to apply the decryption in memory at loading time, i.e., right before the model is used.

The `decrypt_model` algorithm takes the following parameters: the NN model to be decrypted (`model`), and the input data used to measure the accuracy of the decrypted model (`data`). It also needs the `helper` vector created during encryption, which also contains the IDs of the `chosen_weights` as keys, as well as the used `layer_id`. This information is loaded at the beginning of the decryption process (line 2). The decryption procedure is done using the approach explained in the previous section. It simply uses the PUF responses and the encrypted weights to retrieve the original weights via a bitwise XOR operation (lines 5–8).

Note that we test the actual accuracy of the decrypted model at the end of the decryption process. If executed on the target machine (simulated in our PoC by using the same seed for the PUF simulator as for encryption), the accuracy

---

[3] https://pypuf.readthedocs.io.

should match the original accuracy of the model (i.e., before encryption). Otherwise, the accuracy of the NN model will be necessary lower, as planned. The expected incorrect PUF response in the latter case means that the decrypted weight does not match the original weight.

6   Evaluation

We choose four different NN models to evaluate our experiments. We train these models ourselves following TensorFlow tutorials: Two of our models classify images, one is based on the MNIST dataset[4] to detect handwritten digits, and the other one on the Fashion MNIST dataset [18] to detect ten categories of clothing. The other models recognise eight different predefined speech commands [17], and positive or negative sentiment in IMDB reviews [9]. We encrypt a dense layer of each image classification model. For the latter two models, we encrypt one convolutional and one recurrent layer, respectively. For an overview of all experiments, the models we use, and the total number of weights in the layers we encrypt, see Table 1.

Table 1. Overview of the models/layers used in the experiments in Fig. 3.

Exp.	Model Type	Classes	Layer	# Weights
(a)	Image Classification[a]	10 (digits 0–9)	Dense	100 352
(b)	Image Classification[b]	10 (clothing categories)	Dense	100 352
(c)	Audio Recognition[c]	8 (audio commands)	CNN	18 430
(d)	Text Recognition[d]	2 (pos./neg. sentiment)	RNN	16 384

[a]https://www.tensorflow.org/datasets/keras_example
[b]https://www.tensorflow.org/tutorials/keras/classification
[c]https://www.tensorflow.org/tutorials/audio/simple_audio
[d]https://www.tensorflow.org/text/tutorials/text_classification_rnn

6.1   Accuracy

To show the degradation of accuracy in our models due to encryption, we randomly select ten sets of weights containing 40% of the weights per layer to be encrypted. For each of these, we also collect data for subsets including fewer weights at 5% point decrements. For comparison, we also measure the accuracy at 0% encryption, i.e., an unencrypted model. Figure 3 shows the mean of the results of our experiments as well as their standard deviation. Note that these results are only valid for executing the encrypted models without trying to decrypt them.

---

[4] https://www.tensorflow.org/datasets/catalog/mnist

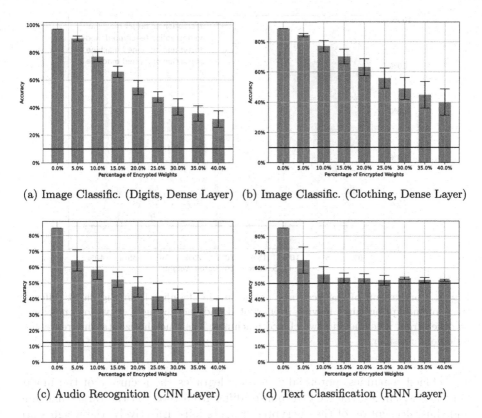

(a) Image Classific. (Digits, Dense Layer)   (b) Image Classific. (Clothing, Dense Layer)

(c) Audio Recognition (CNN Layer)   (d) Text Classification (RNN Layer)

Fig. 3. Mean accuracy drop (and standard deviation) for the models described in Table 1 depending on percentage of encrypted weights for 10 randomly chosen sets of weights each. For comparison, the black horizontal lines represent random classifiers.

For all experiments, the accuracy of the models drops significantly even at 5% encrypted weights and approximates a random classifier (symbolised by the black horizontal line in Fig. 3) at higher percentages of encrypted weights. For example, in Fig. 3d the text classification model's accuracy drops to the value expected for a random classifier at just 10–20%, making the encryption of additional weights unnecessary. By selecting the weights to encrypt carefully, focusing on weights with the most impact, we could decrease the number of weights that must be encrypted in order to achieve the desired level of protection. For more details on this, see Sect. 8.

Figure 4 shows the accuracy of the encrypted model from experiment (a) when used without decryption compared to decryption on various machines. When we decrypt the model on its target machine, we achieve perfect decryption and restore the model's original accuracy. In case the encrypted model is used without decryption, i.e., by extracting it from our software and thus circumventing the execution of the decryption algorithm, the accuracy is lowered (cf. Fig. 3a). Decryption on machines different from the target machine,

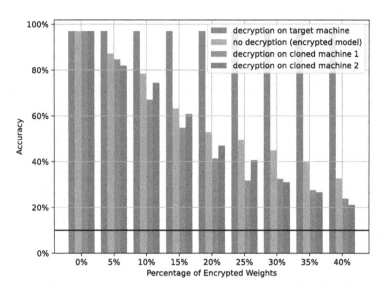

Fig. 4. Comparison of the accuracy of the image classifier from Fig. 3a at different levels of encryption when leaving it encrypted and decrypting it on various machines, i.e., the target machine and two cloned machines. The black horizontal line represents a random classifier.

e.g., cloned machines, potentially further degrades the accuracy of the model. On these machines, the PUF responses differ from those on the target machine and thus, decryption of the encrypted weights fails. Effectively, the weights are encrypted once more, potentially lowering the model's accuracy even further.

6.2   Size Impact

The size of the actual NN model does not change during encryption. Nevertheless, we need to store helper data containing the IDs of the encrypted weights and their respective challenges for the PUF. With our PoC implementation, the size of this data structure increases by 12 bytes per additional encrypted weight. For example, the helper data for the model we use in experiment (a) at 20% encrypted weights, which yields a significant degradation of the model, requires approximately 2.3 MiB of helper data, which could be further reduced by using a more efficient way to identify the weights. The helper data must only be loaded from disk during decryption, and it is not required to load this data into main memory at once. Thus, even on embedded devices, the additional data should not hinder the application of our approach.

7   Discussion

The used one-time key encryption mechanics in the form of Vernam that we apply in this paper achieves *perfect* security in a precise probability-theoretic sense [2, Theorem 12.2]. This means that it is qualified to the best possible extent regarding the secrecy property and the efficiency property of the encryption and decryption algorithms. However, this only holds if the key is (a) truly randomly selected, (b) used only once, and (c) as long as the plaintext. As usual in practice, there are trade-offs in our adaptation to the case of protecting NN models.

In theory, we can meet properties (a) and (c) if the PUF f is injective with domain and range $\{0,1\}^m$, where m is the length of the binary representation of the weights of the NN model N. In practice, we most probably need to replace the "truly random" cipher key by a pseudorandom one, since PUFs are usually not injective and shorter than the required length m. The same applies, for instance, to the Vigenère encryption mechanism [2, Section 13.3], this inevitably results in a less secure encryption. Property (b), on the other hand, can clearly be met, as long as the key generation mechanism does not impose unacceptable overheads.

As our PoC implementation uses a simulated PUF and is not optimised for performance, we did not conduct a performance evaluation. Nevertheless, it is clear that the performance will be heavily influenced by the PUF response time as well as the number of encrypted weights.

It is also apparent that there is a trade-off between performance overhead and security level. This is determined by the desired drop in accuracy on the one hand and the type of encryption on the other. If the model is only decrypted once after loading (as per our PoC implementation), then the PUF response time does not affect the runtime, only the loading time is affected. If we use a more secure approach instead where each individual weight is decrypted on demand for each processed input, and then encrypted again immediately after use (possibly with a new key), then this will clearly have a negative impact in the NN model's performance. At the same time, the resulting protection would have better resistance to sophisticated (dynamic) reverse engineering attacks.

In our PoC, we select weights at random and show that the encryption of around 20% of the weights is enough to obtain a sufficient degradation in the accuracy of the NN models, and thus being able to apply the proposed copy protection against static attacks. To offer protection against dynamic attacks as outlined in the previous paragraph, but without affecting the performance significantly, one could potentially encrypt/decrypt a substantially smaller number of weight for each input processed by the NN model. This can still degrade the accuracy of the NN model enough (see, e.g., [6, 15]). We plan to investigate this alternative in future research.

A final point that should be noted is that if attackers can somehow query the PUF on the target machine to get the needed responses, then they can obviously decrypt the network. There are, however, known ways to make PUFs resistant to this type of attacks (see, e.g., [1, 10]). Additionally, we could use obfuscation techniques so that an attacker cannot easily identify where each PUF response is used. There is also the possibility of considering Trusted Execution Environments (TEEs) for key operations or homomorphic encryption. Again, this needs to be investigated in future work and will necessary involve a trade-off between security and performance.

8   Related Work

Protecting the IP in NN models is of course not a completely new idea. Indeed, several alternative methods already exist. In this section, we will discuss the most relevant work in this sense.

We can identify two main approaches depending on how IP protection is applied: (i) by means of different obfuscation techniques [7,20] that make it sufficiently harder for an attacker to recover the original model, and (ii) by using cryptography [3,8,12] to either encrypt the whole model, individual layers or, as in our case, individual weights. In the remainder of this section, we discuss each of these related techniques.

The Goldstein et al. [7] have shown that a good level of protection may be achieved by applying various alterations to the structure of convolutional filters in Deep Convolutional Neural Networks (DCNNs). To revert the applied obfuscation, a secret key is needed. If an incorrect key is provided, the resulting model will have a significantly lower accuracy than the original model.

Rakin et al. [13] explore the effects of applying bit flips induced by Rowhammer attacks to a neural network. The authors use these bit flips to attack a model and render it useless for other users. While this idea is not directly related to our work, Zhao et al. [20] use a similar technique to protect neural networks. They propose to calculate an error mask based on DRAM restore values that pose as a unique physical property of individual DRAM modules. As such, the authors are able to create an error mask that is bound to a specific DRAM module. They proceed to use this error mask while training a neural network. The resulting model is then bound to the DRAM module that will yield the correct error mask. If executed on another DRAM module, the accuracy of the model is significantly lower than the accuracy of the original model. The key difference to our approach is that their model needs to be individually trained for each piece of hardware it runs on while our work can be applied to any pre-trained model.

Cai et al. [3] apply encryption to only a small portion of the weights. They apply the proposed encryption using a pre-calculated set of secret keys that are stored in a separate key storage. The authors show that encrypting only a small portion of the weights is enough to achieve a sufficient level of protection. In contrast to our work, they rely on a set of keys that, if known to an attacker, can be used to run the network at any arbitrary machine whereas our approach is bound to specific hardware by using a PUF to generate secret keys while encrypting and decrypting the model.

Making use of FPGAs to accelerate the execution time of neural networks is a well known method. Guo et al. [8] propose to directly integrate their protection into such an accelerator FPGA. They make use of a PUF that only yields the correct results when executed on the correct FPGA. While their method seems very promising, particularly regarding the low performance overhead associated with the proposed protection, the solution is specifically tailored to convolutional NNs running on FPGA hardware.

Finally, Pan et al. [12] use an Anderson PUF to incrementally encrypt layers of a NN to efficiently bind it to specific hardware. They focus on analysing the effectiveness of the protection to counteract fine-tuning attacks. This is a type of attack that tries to approximate the original model from the obfuscated one by making use of a fraction of the original training dataset. A key difference to our approach is that they aim to render the behaviour of the protected model equivalent to a random classifier. In contrast, our work has identified that obfuscating only a small fraction of the weights is enough to achieve a good level of protection against software piracy. Since we can limit the loss in accuracy to a few percentage points, in theory we should be able to make our approach more stealthy, which would in turn give us an advantage w.r.t. the fine-tuning attacks considered in their work. The conjecture is that then it is not immediately obvious for an attacker how the encrypted NN model produces the drop in performance. This still needs to be confirmed by future research, though.

9   Conclusion

In this work, we presented a method to protect intellectual property in neural network models from piracy. The main advantage of our approach is that NN models cannot simply be copied to replicated machines, thus requiring reverse engineering not just for the hardware but also the NN models. We evaluated our method using different NN models and showed that they can be bound to unique hardware properties in such a way that copying an NN model to another machine renders it useless. Furthermore, this complicates a static analysis, since without knowledge of the properties of the target hardware, i.e., PUF responses, this mechanism cannot simply be removed.

A further step and planned future work is to make this protection more robust against dynamic analysis. The current PoC implements the decryption after loading, i.e., the entire model is decrypted and then stored decrypted in main memory. A possible improvement in this respect would be to decrypt only individual weights that are currently being used and then encrypt them again, or to integrate this mechanism into a trusted execution environment. In addition, it is also necessary to analyse and optimise performance and subsequently achieve a good trade-off between performance and security, i.e., the number of weights to be encrypted.

References

1. Al-Meer, A., Al-Kuwari, S.: Physical unclonable functions (PUF) for IoT devices. ACM Comput. Surv. 55(14s), 1–31 (2023). https://doi.org/10.1145/3591464
2. Biskup, J.: Security in Computing Systems - Challenges, Approaches and Solutions. Springer, Heidelberg (2009). https://doi.org/10.1007/978-3-540-78442-5

3. Cai, Y., Chen, X., Tian, L., Wang, Y., Yang, H.: Enabling secure NVM-based in-memory neural network computing by sparse fast gradient encryption. IEEE Trans. Comput. **69**(11), 1596–1610 (2020). https://doi.org/10.1109/TC.2020.3017870

4. Curtis, D.: Software piracy and copyright protection. In: Proceedings of WESCON 1994, pp. 199–203 (1994). https://doi.org/10.1109/WESCON.1994.403604

5. Fischer, B.: Design of a rowhammer-based unique hardware identification mechanism. Master's thesis, University of Applied Sciences Upper Austria, Hagenberg Campus (2023). https://permalink.obvsg.at/fho/AC16895522

6. Frantar, E., Alistarh, D.: SparseGPT: massive language models can be accurately pruned in one-shot (2023). https://arxiv.org/abs/2301.00774

7. Goldstein, B.F., Patil, V.C., Ferreira, V.C., Nery, A.S., França, F.M.G., Kundu, S.: Preventing DNN model IP theft via hardware obfuscation. IEEE J. Emerg. Sel. Top. Circuits Syst. **11**(2), 267–277 (2021). https://doi.org/10.1109/JETCAS.2021.3076151

8. Guo, Q., Ye, J., Gong, Y., Hu, Y., Li, X.: PUF based pay-per-device scheme for IP protection of CNN model. In: 2018 IEEE 27th Asian Test Symposium (ATS), pp. 115–120 (2018). https://doi.org/10.1109/ATS.2018.00032

9. Maas, A.L., Daly, R.E., Pham, P.T., Huang, D., Ng, A.Y., Potts, C.: Learning word vectors for sentiment analysis. In: Proceedings of the 49th Annual Meeting of the Association for Computational Linguistics: Human Language Technologies, Portland, Oregon, USA, pp. 142–150. Association for Computational Linguistics (2011). https://www.aclweb.org/anthology/P11-1015

10. McGrath, T., Bagci, I.E., Wang, Z.M., Roedig, U., Young, R.J.: A PUF taxonomy. Appl. Phys. Rev. **6**(1), 011303 (2019). https://doi.org/10.1063/1.5079407

11. Oliynyk, D., Mayer, R., Rauber, A.: I know what you trained last summer: a survey on stealing machine learning models and defences. ACM Comput. Surv. **55**(14s) (2023). https://doi.org/10.1145/3595292

12. Pan, Q., Dong, M., Ota, K., Wu, J.: Device-bind key-storageless hardware AI model IP protection: a PUF and permute-diffusion encryption-enabled approach (2022). https://arxiv.org/abs/2212.11133

13. Rakin, A.S., He, Z., Fan, D.: Bit-flip attack: crushing neural network with progressive bit search (2019). https://arxiv.org/abs/1903.12269

14. Reavis Conner, K., Rumelt, R.P.: Software piracy: an analysis of protection strategies. Manag. Sci. **37**(2), 125–139 (1991). https://doi.org/10.1287/mnsc.37.2.125

15. Ruospo, A., Gavarini, G., Bragaglia, I., Traiola, M., Bosio, A., Sanchez, E.: Selective hardening of critical neurons in deep neural networks. In: 2022 25th International Symposium on Design and Diagnostics of Electronic Circuits and Systems (DDECS), pp. 136–141 (2022). https://doi.org/10.1109/DDECS54261.2022.9770168

16. Suh, G.E., Devadas, S.: Physical unclonable functions for device authentication and secret key generation. In: Proceedings of the 44th Annual Design Automation Conference, DAC 2007, pp. 9–14. Association for Computing Machinery, New York (2007). https://doi.org/10.1145/1278480.1278484

17. Warden, P.: Speech commands: a dataset for limited-vocabulary speech recognition (2018). https://arxiv.org/abs/1804.03209

18. Xiao, H., Rasul, K., Vollgraf, R.: Fashion-MNIST: a novel image dataset for benchmarking machine learning algorithms (2017). https://arxiv.org/abs/1708.07747

19. Xu, K., Wang, Z.: The design of a neural network-based adaptive control method for robotic arm trajectory tracking. Neural Comput. Appl. **35**, 8785–8795 (2022). https://doi.org/10.1007/s00521-022-07646-y
20. Zhao, L., Zhang, Y., Yang, J.: AEP: an error-bearing neural network accelerator for energy efficiency and model protection. In: 2017 IEEE/ACM International Conference on Computer-Aided Design (ICCAD), pp. 1047–1053 (2017). https://doi.org/10.1109/ICCAD.2017.8203897

Author Index

Printed in the United States
by Baker & Taylor Publisher Services